BRICK
CARS AND TRUCKS

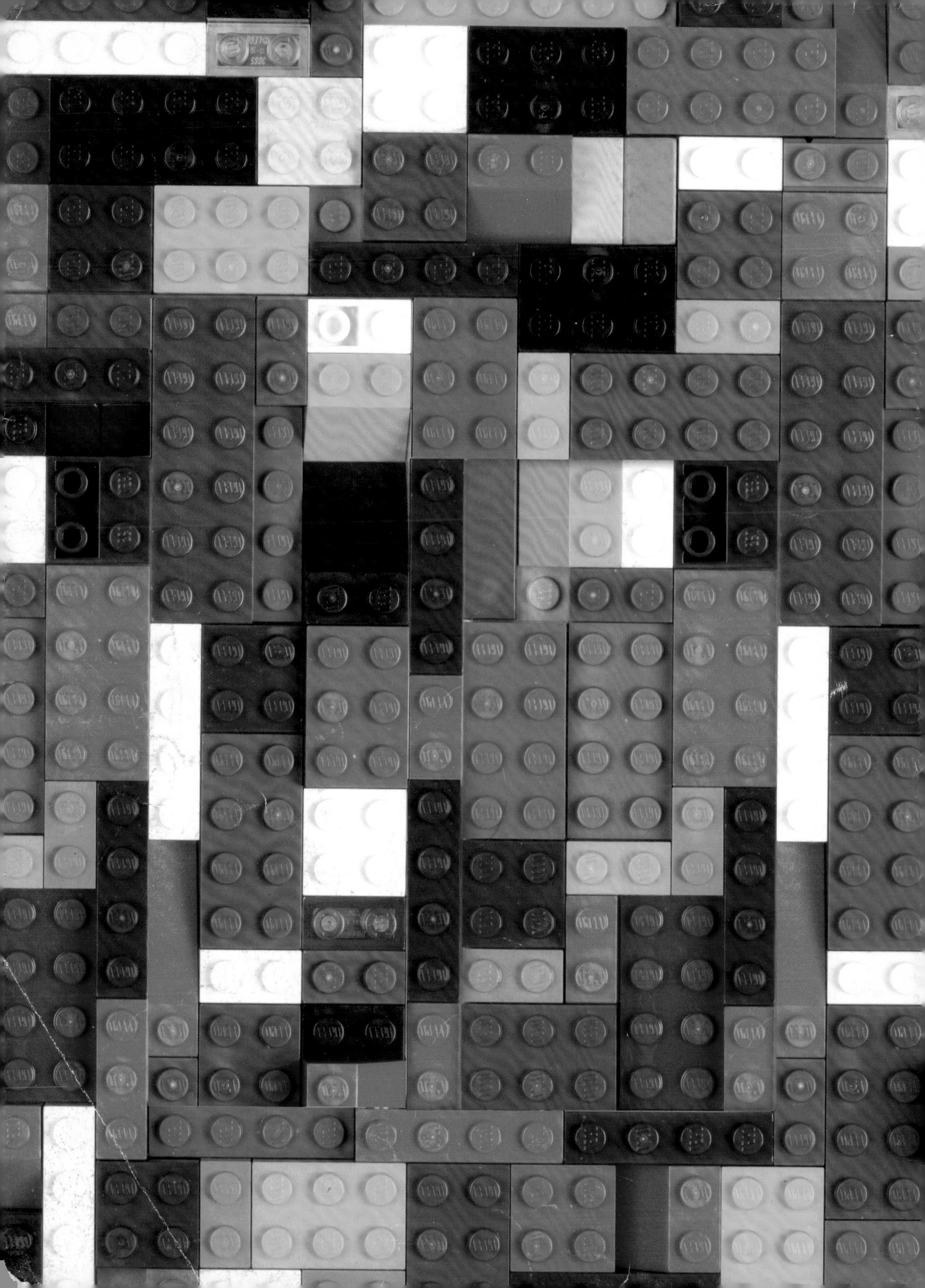

BRICK
CARS AND TRUCKS

CLEVER AND CREATIVE IDEAS TO MAKE FROM CLASSIC LEGO®

WARREN ELSMORE

Quintet Publishing, an imprint of The Quarto Group

First edition for the United States and Canada
published in 2016 by Barron's Educational Series, Inc.

All inquiries should be addressed to:
Barron's Educational Series, Inc.
250 Wireless Boulevard
Hauppauge, NY 11788
www.barronseduc.com

Library of Congress Control Number: 2015949331
ISBN 978-1-4380-0881-3
QTT.BKITC

This book was conceived, designed, and produced by
Quintet Publishing, an imprint of The Quarto Group
The Old Brewery, 6 Blundell Street,
London N7 9BH, United Kingdom
T (0)207700 6700
www.QuartoKnows.com

Photographer: Neal Grundy
Designer: Gareth Butterworth
Art Director: Michael Charles
Project Editor: Caroline Elliker
Editorial Director: Emma Bastow
Publisher: Mark Searle

9 8 7 6 5 4 3

Printed in China by C & C Offset Printing Co Ltd.

welcome to BRICK CARS AND TRUCKS

When I work at public events building LEGO® models, I'm often asked the same question: "Why does LEGO produce all these special parts now? Back in my day it was all just bricks." Well, to prove that you can create anything from just bricks, we decided to write this book.

The idea that The LEGO Company has changed its kit and that specialist pieces are new isn't really correct. Even back in 1950, when you could buy a box of basic 2 x 4 bricks, The LEGO Company still sold special doors and windows! Wheels did take a little longer to appear, but they have been a staple of any LEGO model for 50 years now. So when we decided to build a model out of "basic bricks" we first had to decide what a "basic brick" was.

For this book, my team took their inspiration from the LEGO CLASSIC series of sets. Each of these sets provides exactly what those visitors I meet at public events ask about: a big box of LEGO bricks. Of course, not every brick is a standard 2 x 4 brick, or 2 x 2 plate, or 1 x 3 slope—but everyone should recognize the collection of LEGO pieces.

Color is important for some of these vehicles, although the colored bricks available in the CLASSIC boxes were not always the ones we wanted—that's when having multiple CLASSIC boxes comes in handy! Of course, when you're building these vehicles yourself you can change the colors according to the bricks you have.

Finally, if you want to build one of the models in this book but don't have exactly the right pieces already—don't worry! We spent lots of time trying to decide if we should use one type of slope over another, but in the end it's a very personal decision. If you decide that your vehicle looks better with a different piece, that's great! Remember, there is no right or wrong with LEGO. As long as you've enjoyed building the model, then that's all that matters.

—Warren Elsmore

contents

Dragster 6
Monster Truck 8
Garbage Truck 10
Tractor Trailer Cab 12
Tractor Trailer 14
Convertible 16
Tow Truck 18
School Bus 20
VW Camper 22
Forklift 25
Mobile Crane 28
Sports Car 30
Digger 32
Snowplow 34
Cement Mixer 37
Fire Engine 40
Police Car 42
Race Car 44
Car Carrier 46
Quad Bike 48
Rolls-Royce 50
Tanker Truck 52
Tractor 54
Bulldozer 57
Dump Truck 60
Ford Model T 62
Cherry Picker 64
Smart Car 66
Mini Cooper 68
Taxi 70
Tuk Tuk 72
VW Beetle 74
Vintage Car 77
Flying Car 80
Go Kart 82
Moon Buggy 84
Double-Decker Bus 86
Ice Cream Truck 89
Jeep 92
Hummer 94
Credits 96

dragster

Drag racing is a popular motor sport all over the world. Instead of racing around a track, the cars compete in a straight line. So while they come in a variety of shapes and classes, they're all built for speed! We've chosen to make a classic one with a very long, low nose, and a higher back end. To help build our long-nosed chassis, we've used a collection of two plates in a row, with the front wheel axle far ahead of the center. It's ready to be taken for a spin!

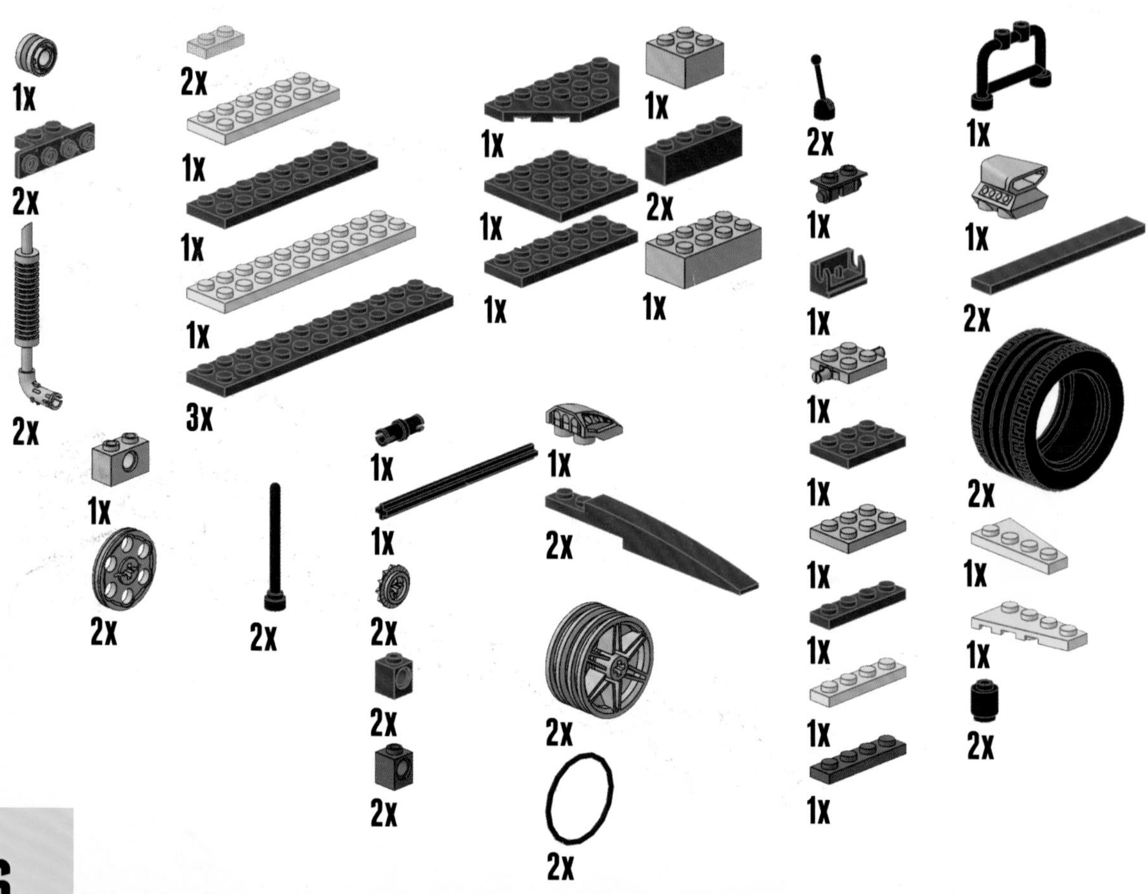

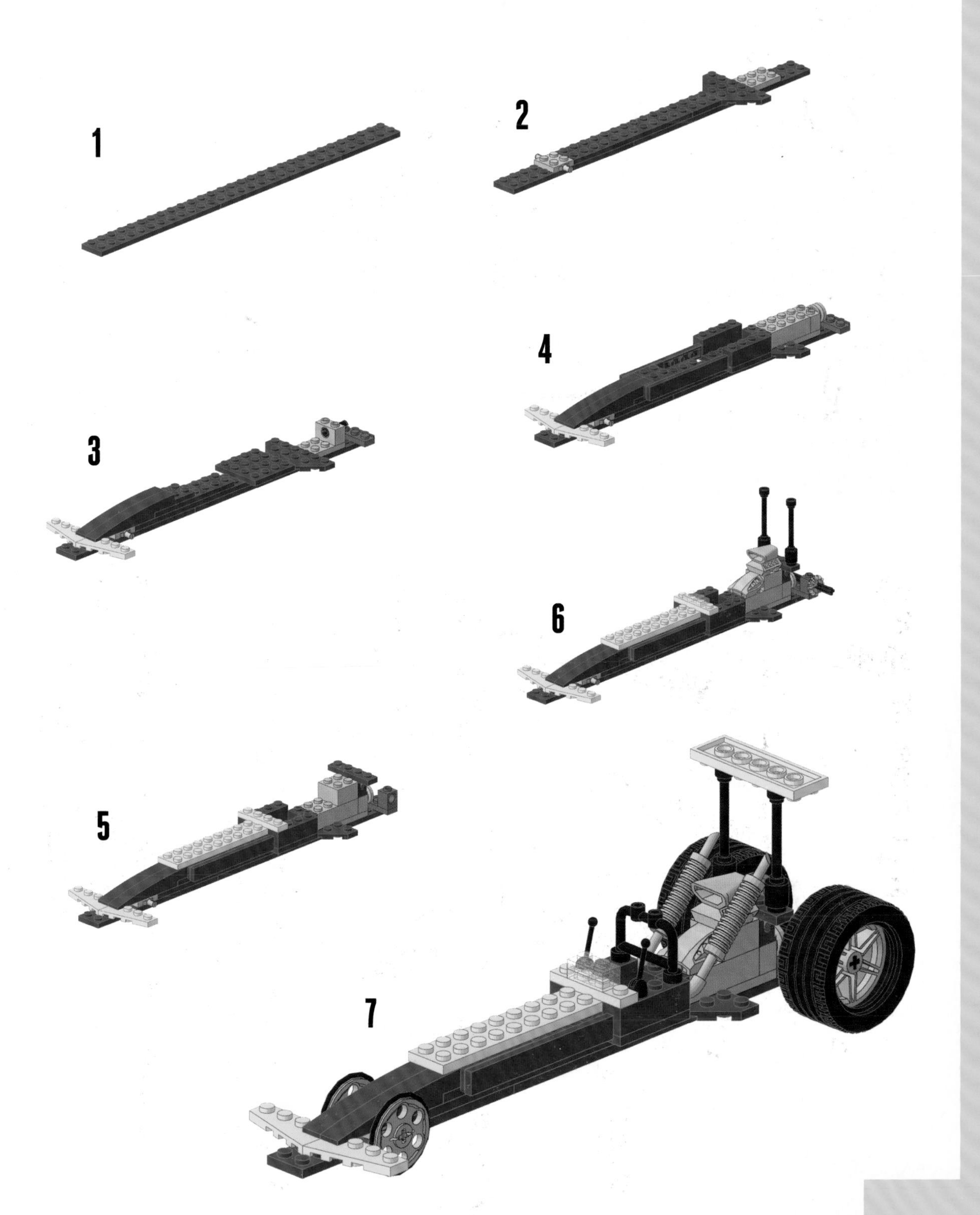
1
2
3
4
5
6
7

monster truck

Monster trucks are basically glorified pick-up trucks, with massively oversized tires and super suspension. They tend to be used for entertainment, where drivers have loads of fun crushing motor homes in front of a cheering crowd. Their huge wheels can make them a bit unstable, so driving them takes a lot of skill. For our monster truck we've used the 4 x 10 chassis to give it a good solid base for stability. Wheel arches sit over the bigger wheels and tires. By setting the axles on several plates under the wheel arches, the suspension can travel a long way—a must when bouncing over other cars.

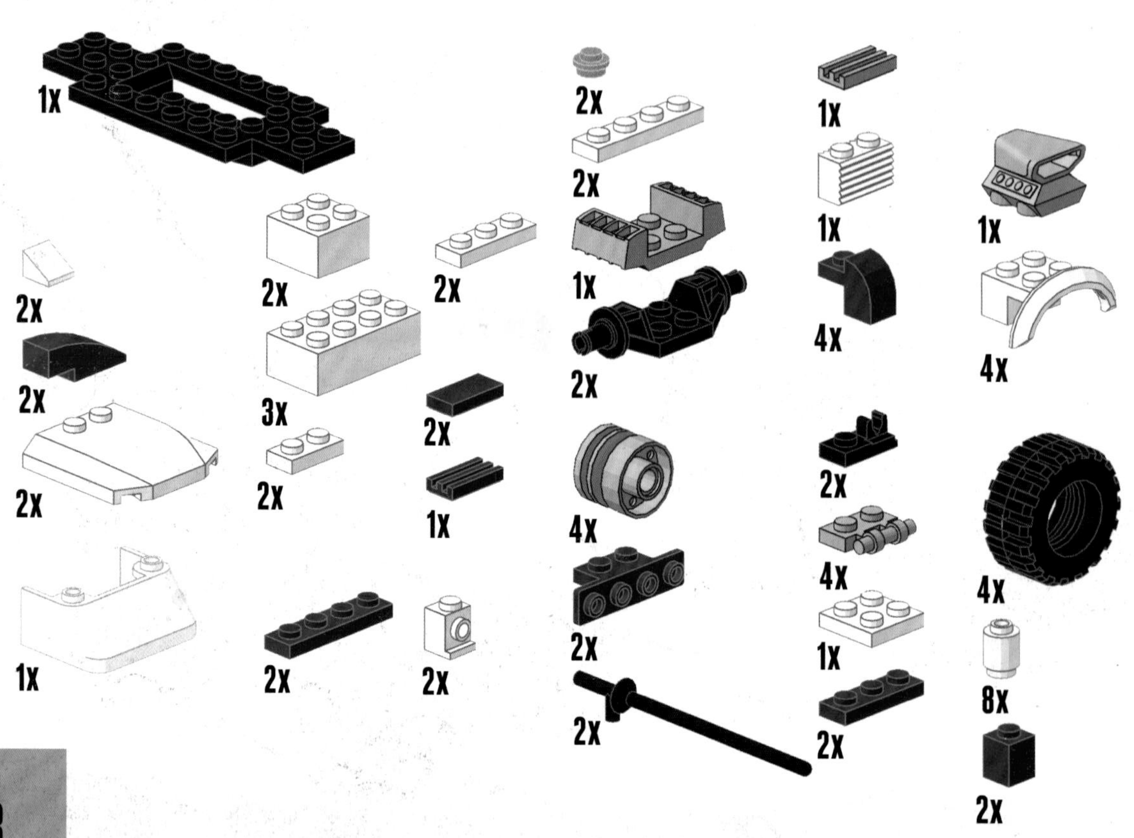

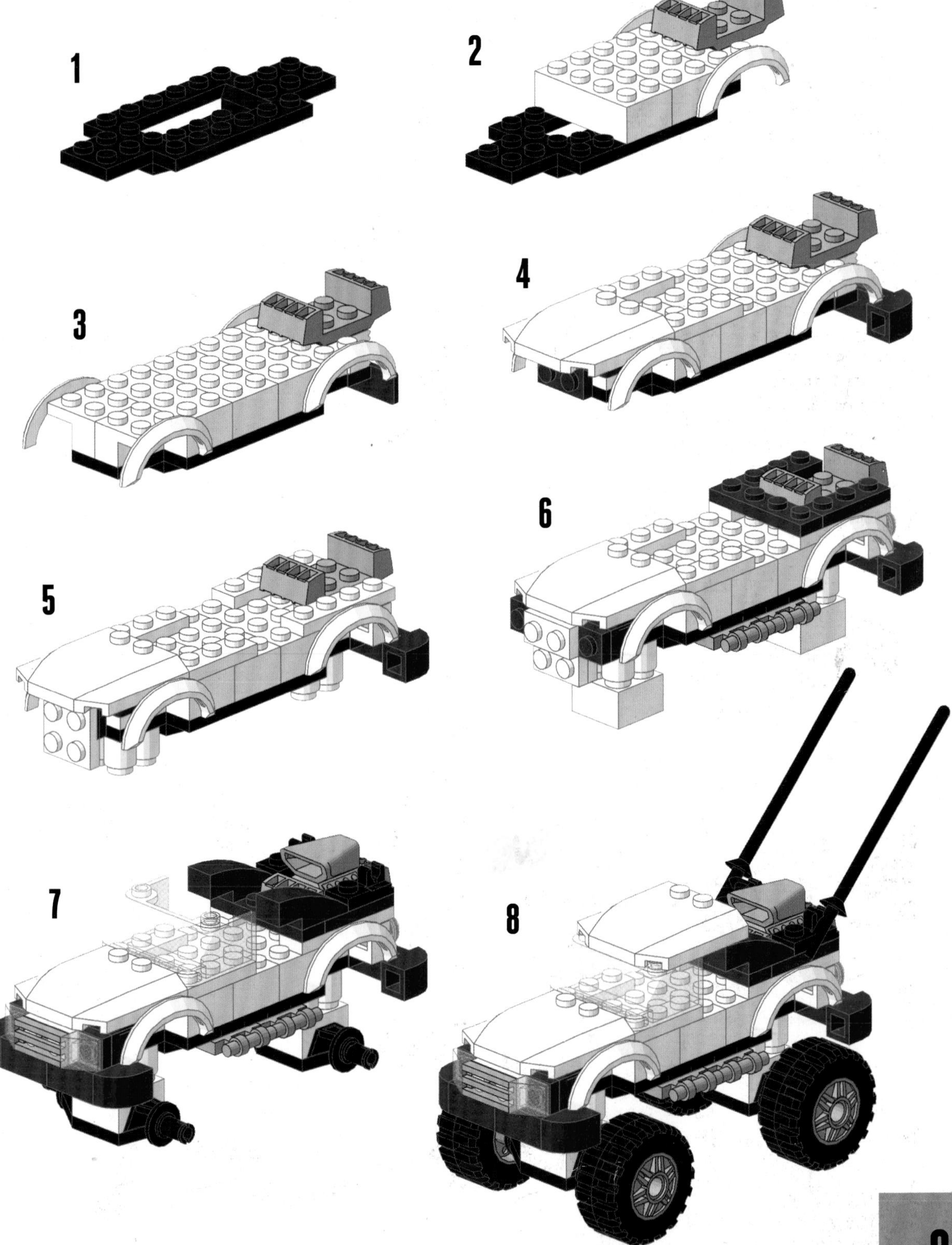
1
2
3
4
5
6
7
8

garbage truck

You can usually smell this truck before you can see it, as it drives around our neighborhoods collecting trash. Some empty the trash cans into their compactors by lifting them on arms over the tractor cab. Others, like ours, lift their arms into the back of the truck. We've used 1 x 2 x 3 panels, alternated with bricks, to show the corrugated sides of the truck body, and a 1 x 2 x 2 ladder piece for the large front radiator. In case you haven't smelled it coming, use the 1 x 1 transparent orange round plates on top to create flashing warning lights!

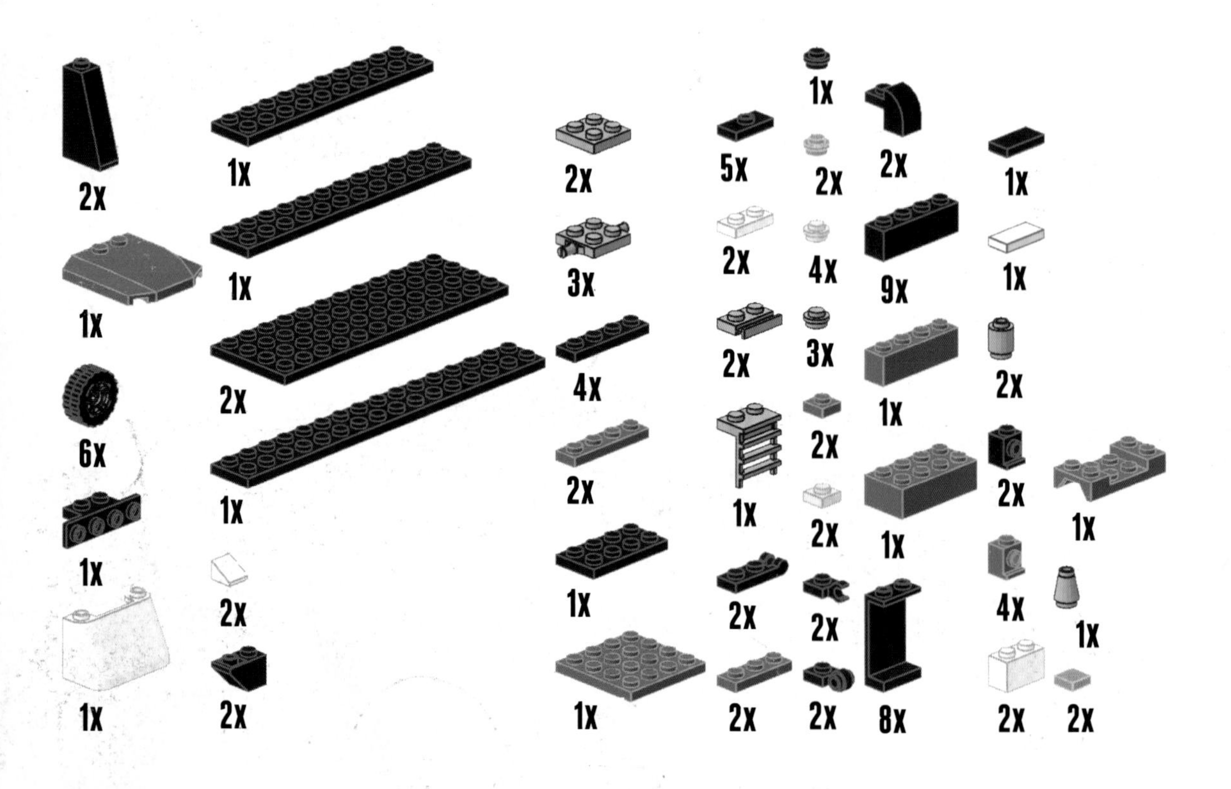

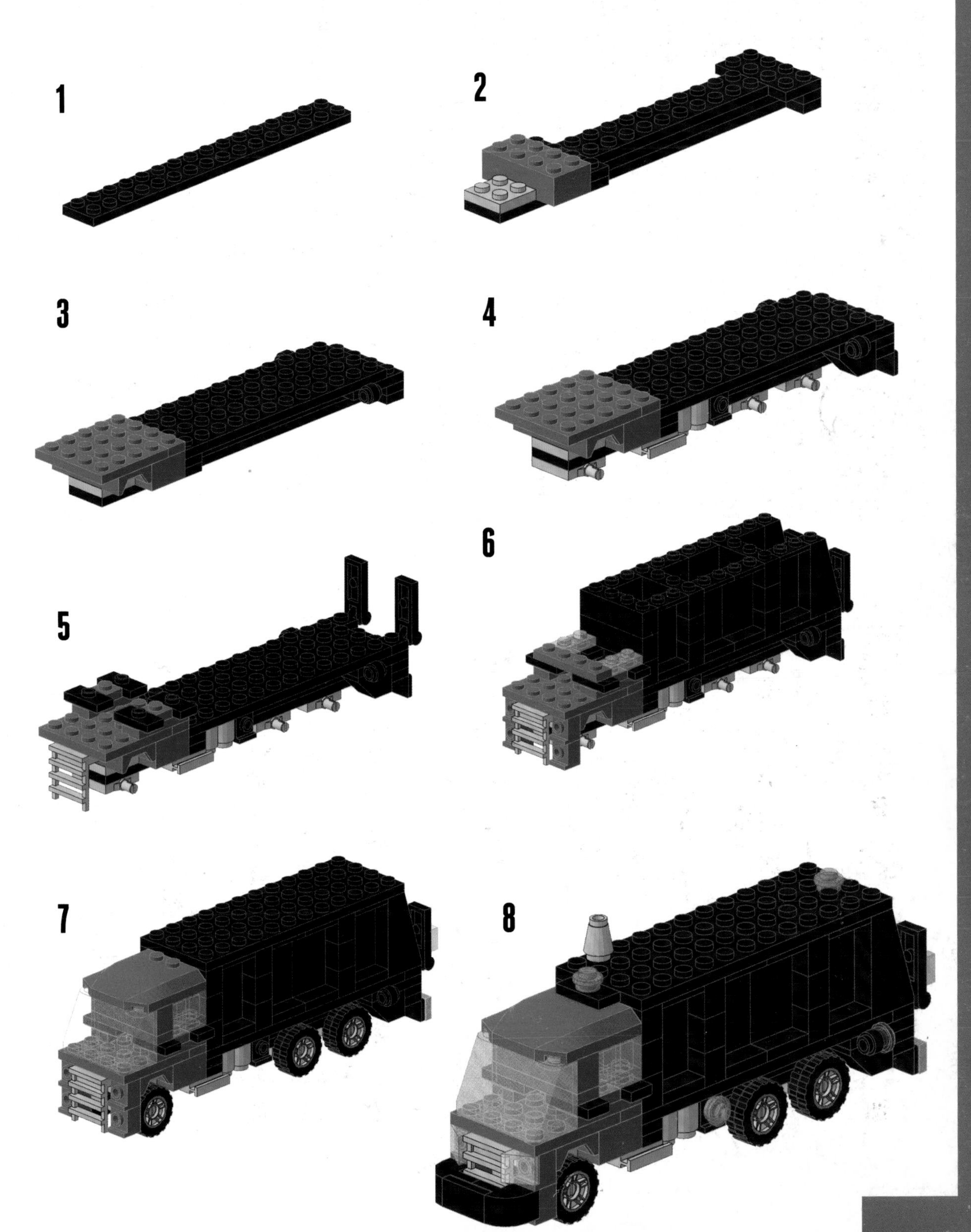
1
2
3
4
5
6
7
8

tractor trailer cab

Honk honk! Heavy load coming through! To pull such a weighty cargo you need a strong cab up front, with three sets of wheels to make it easier to handle. The tractor trailer cab is a powerful vehicle built to pull several trailer units at once. They travel long distances all over the world, from Argentina, Australia, and Mexico to the United States and Canada, carrying huge loads of fuel and other cargo. Many cabs have a place for the driver to sleep on long trips.

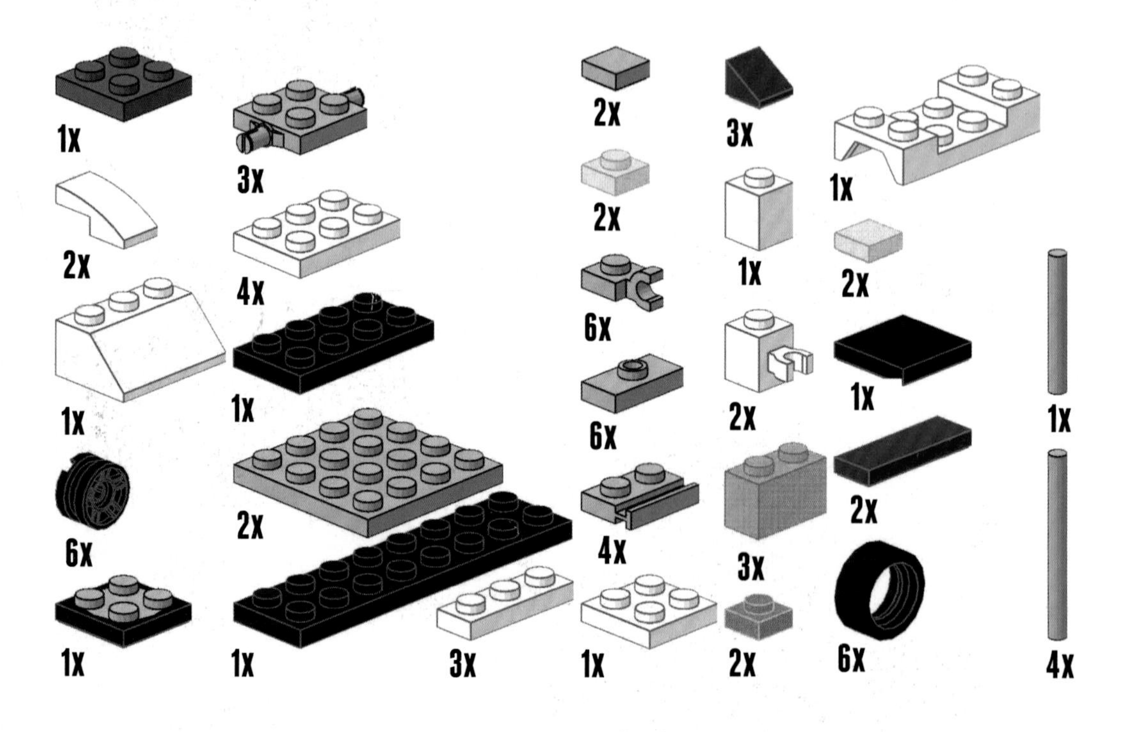

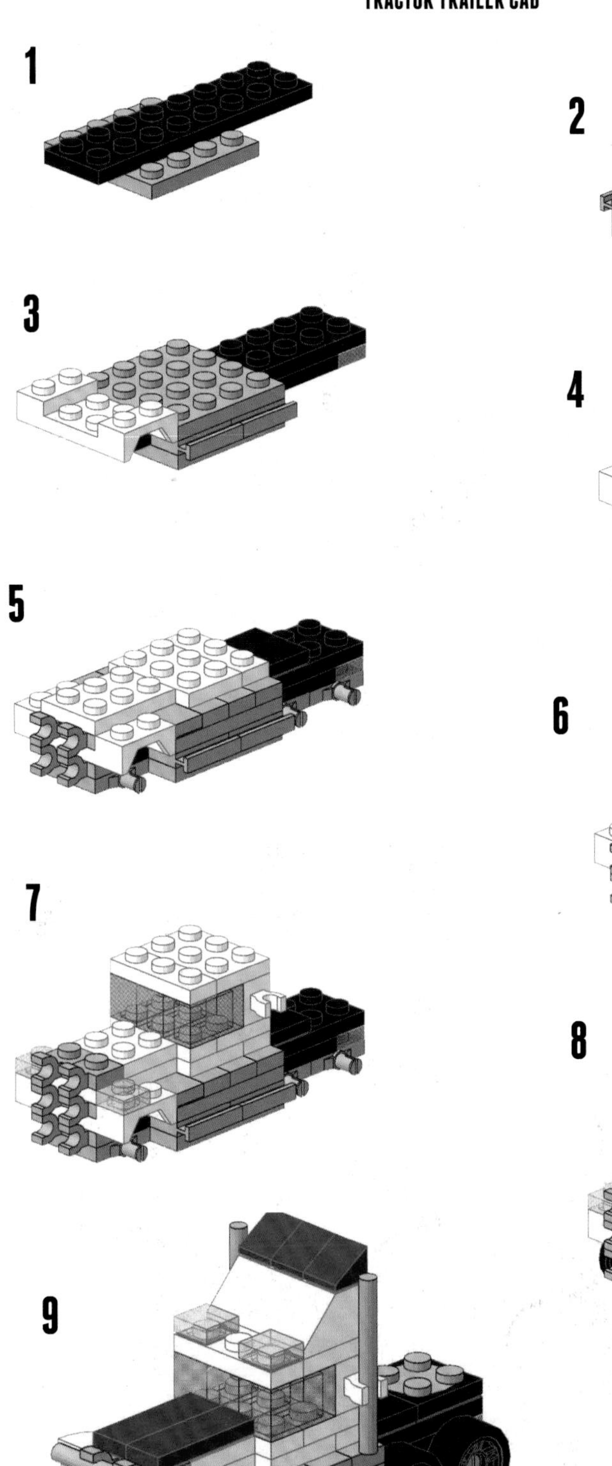

1
3
5
7
9

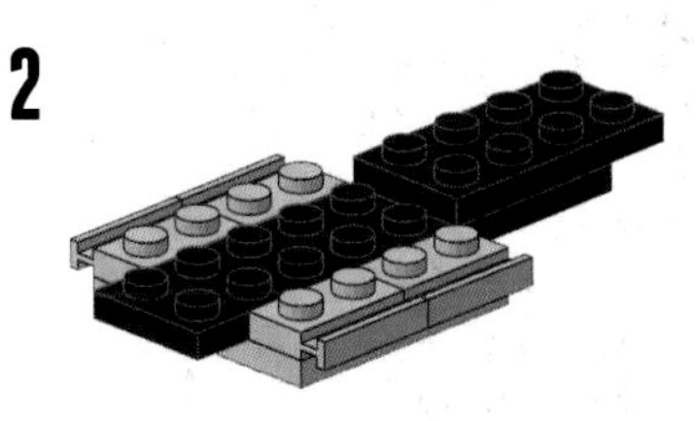

2

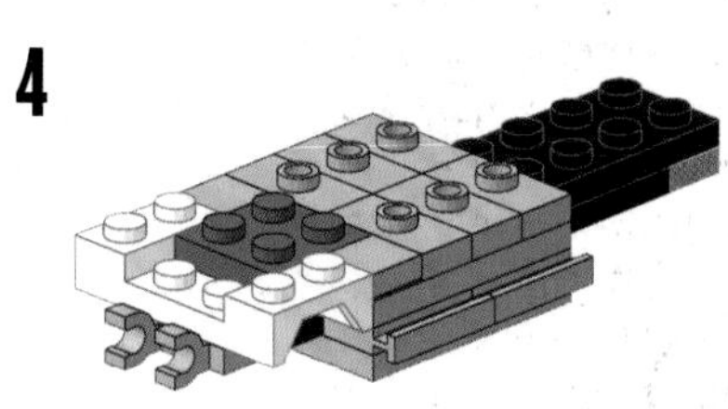

4

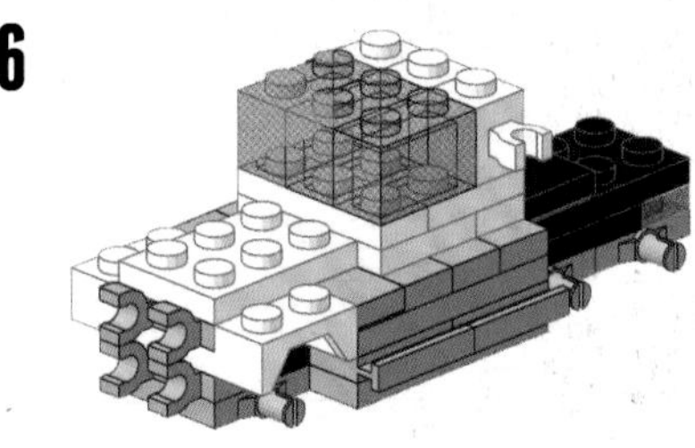

6

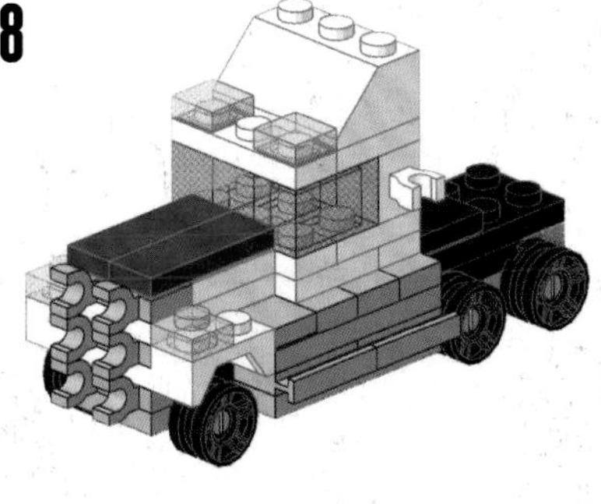

8

tractor trailer

Our trailer unit has two axles, but semi-trailers can have up to four rear axles. The front of this trailer connects to a king-pin on the back of the tractor unit—the fifth wheel. In some parts of the world, these trailers are connected to another trailer being towed behind on a drawbar. In this way, a single tractor unit can pull as many as six trailers at once! There are many names for this arrangement—a triple, a road train, and a B-double being the most well-known.

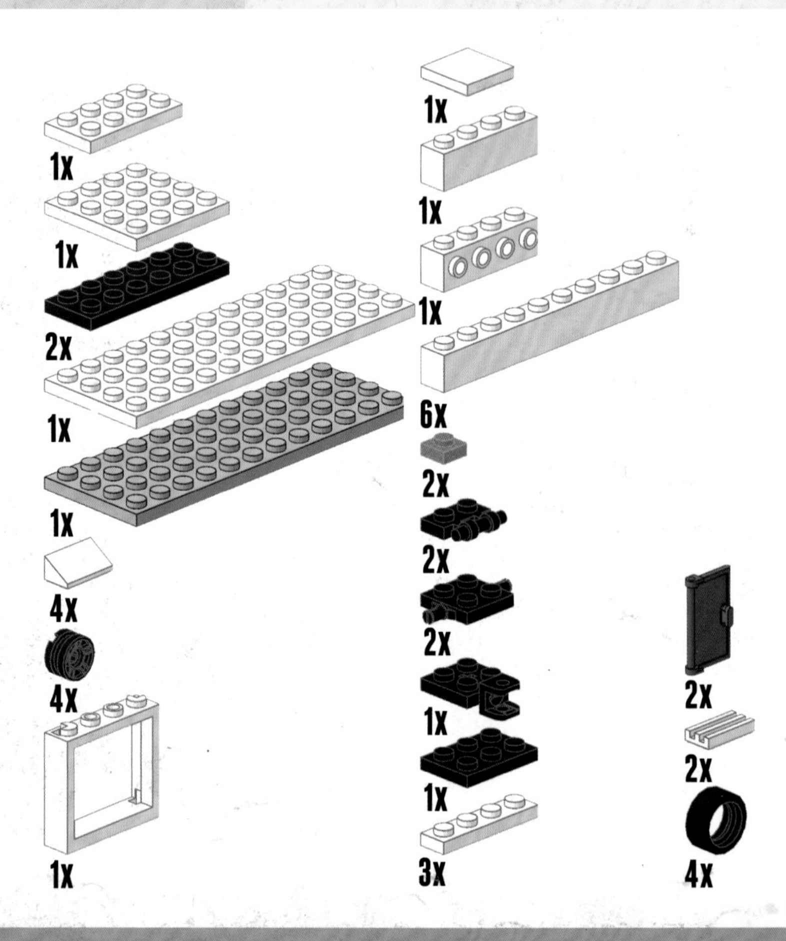

1

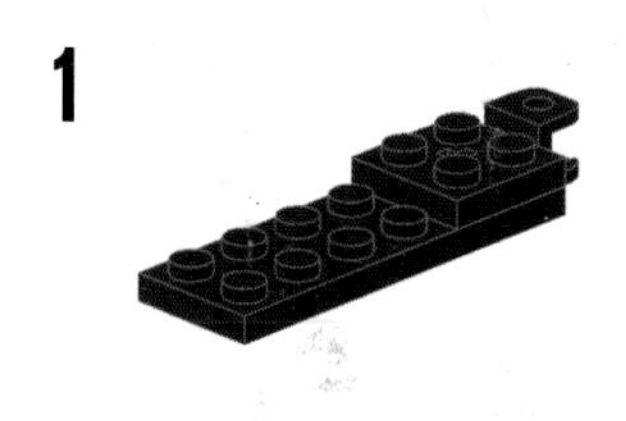

2

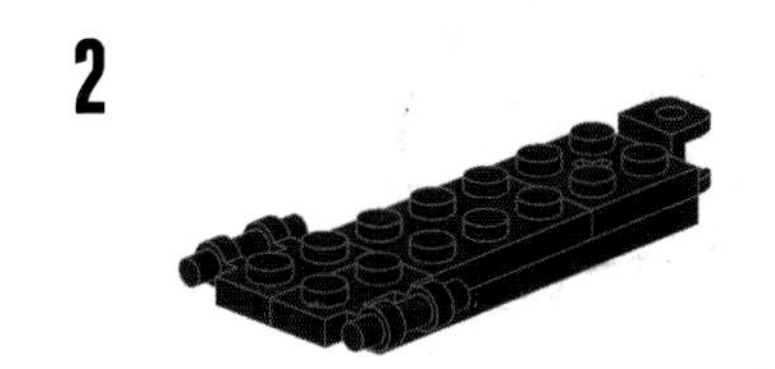

3

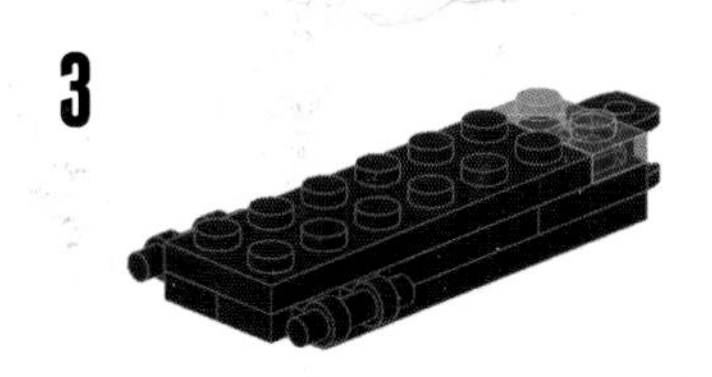

4

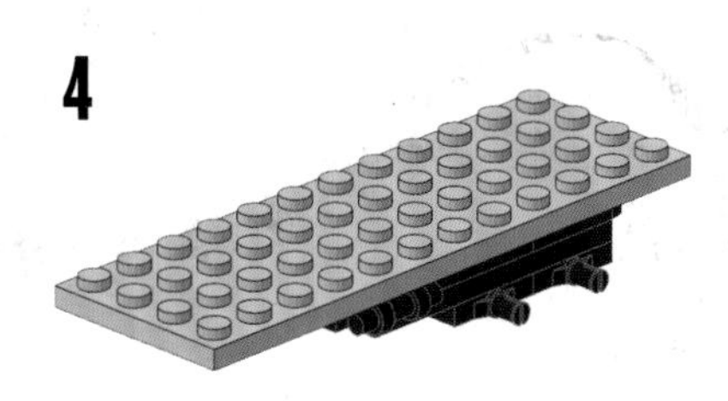

5

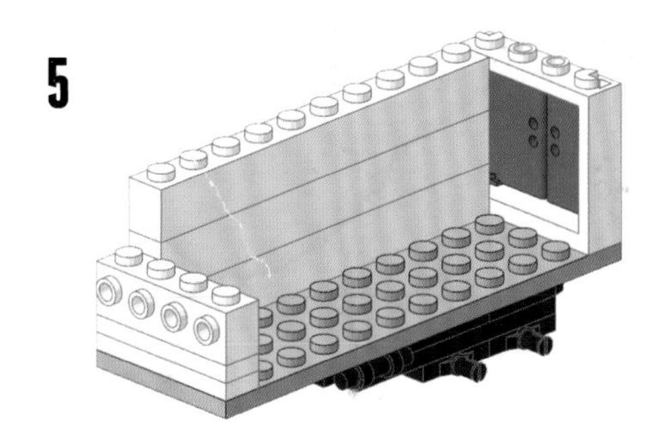

6

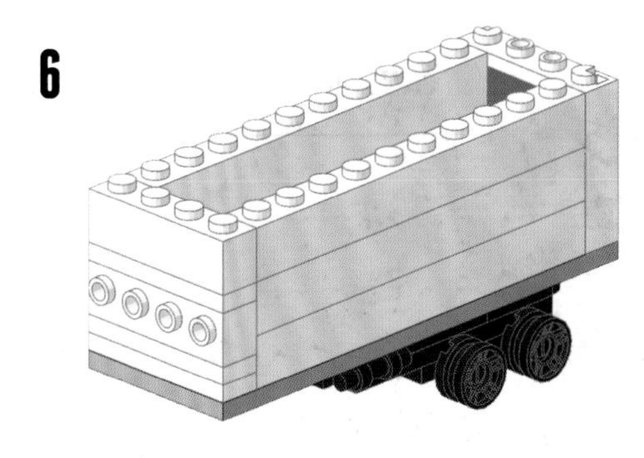

7

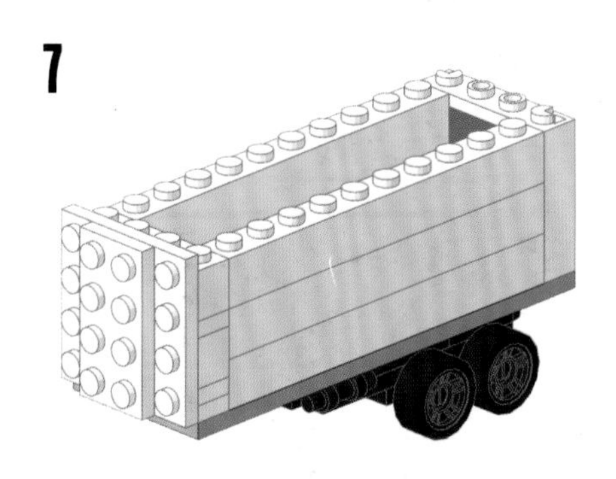

8

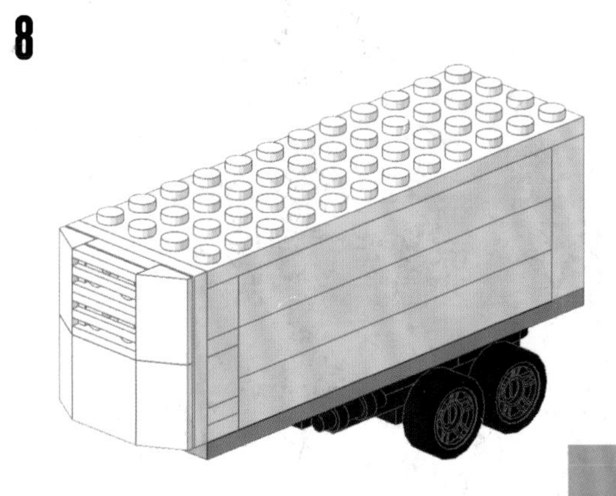

convertible

The sun is shining, the weather is hot ... it's time to turn the radio up and put the roof down! A convertible is the car of summer, able to switch to being an open-air model in no time. Most have fabric roofs with a built-in foldable rear windshield and they can have two or four seats. The low-slung, stylish body is designed to turn heads. This cute yellow car is an homage to the Ferrari and Lamborghini. The fold-down roof is hidden under a black cover behind the seats.

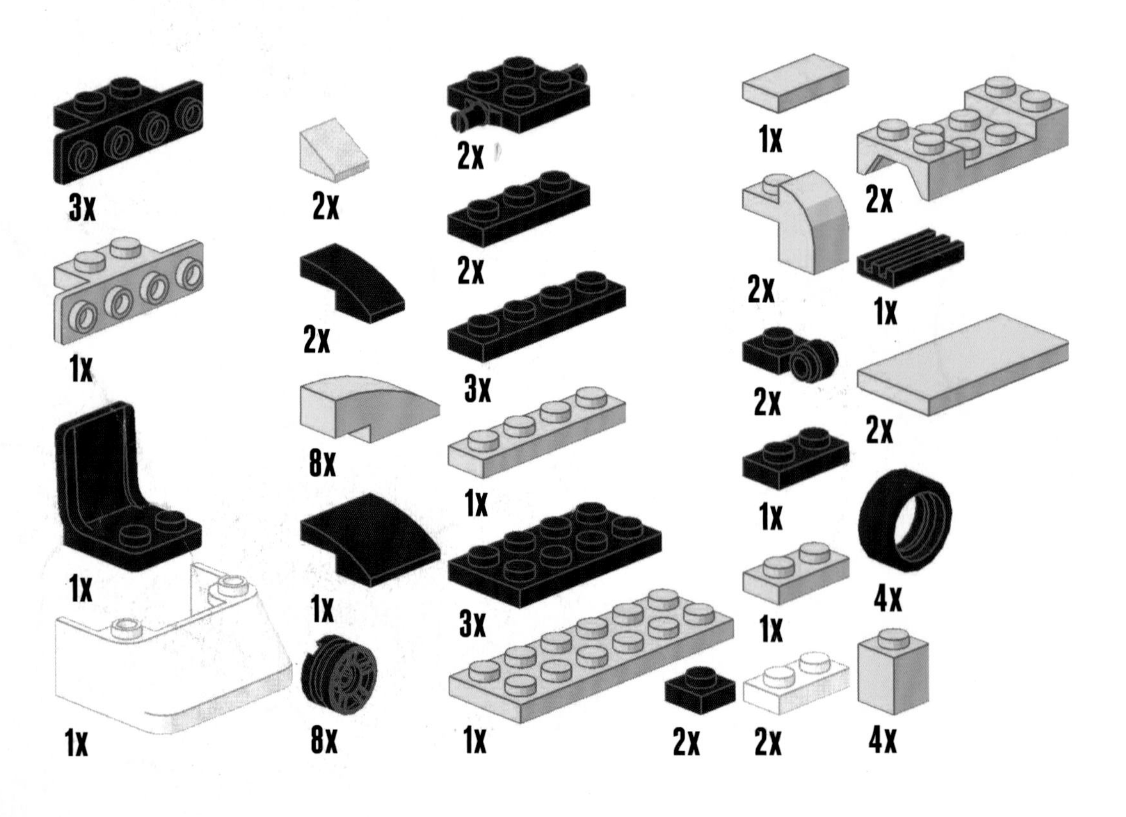

1

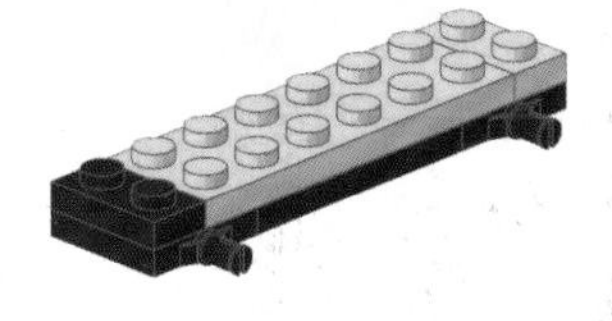

2

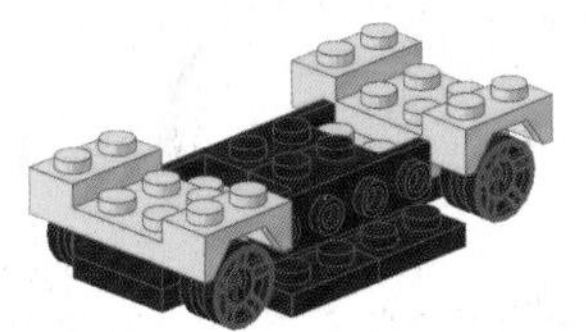

3

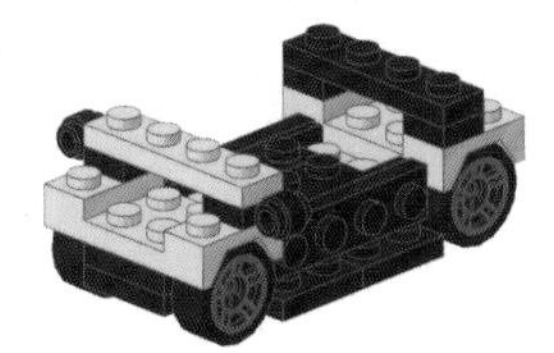

4

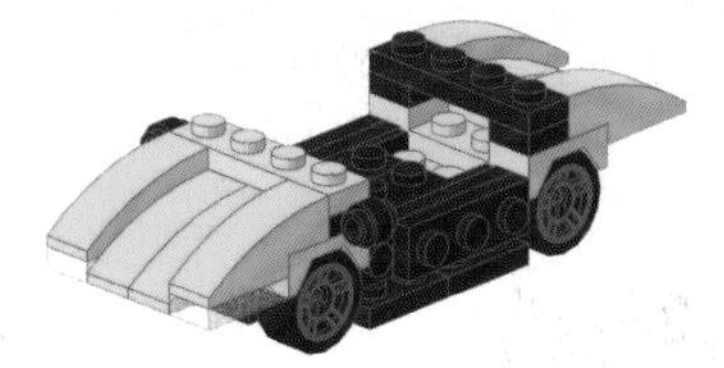

5

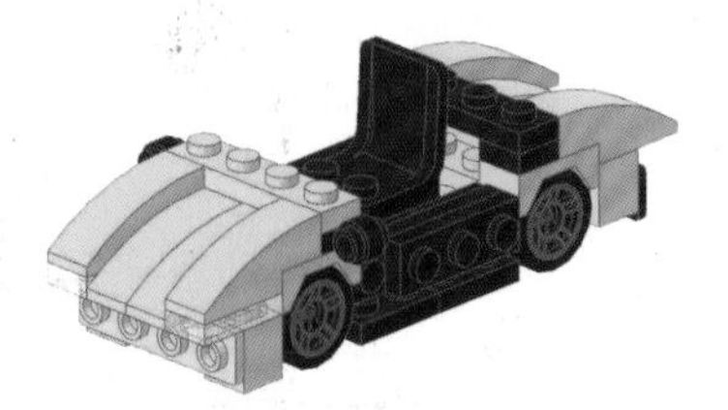

6

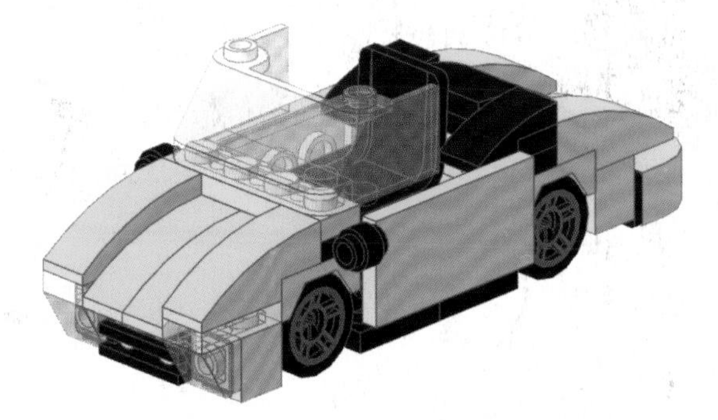

tow truck

Tow trucks are pretty handy to have around in an emergency. The winches and bars at the back are designed to connect and secure any vehicles that are in trouble. This means they're perfect for moving broken down cars or towing any that are illegally parked. They can even recover those stuck in a muddy field or flooded area. We've used a 4 x 4 curved hood piece for the large front of the truck. The rear equipment, for holding the wheels, is held in place by a 1 x 2 plate click hinge. Link this with two 1 x 4 long plates using a 2 x 2 double jumper.

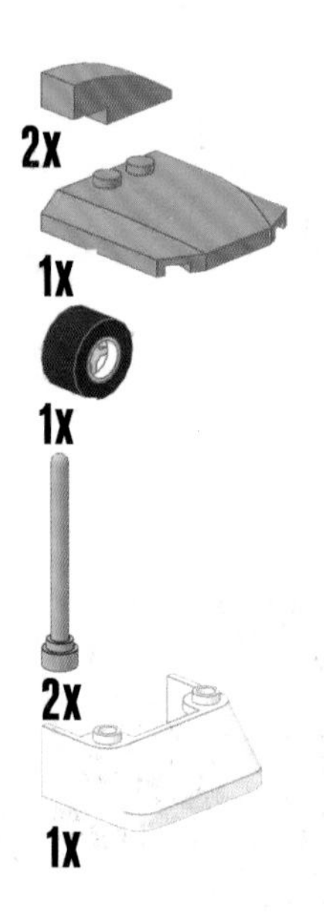

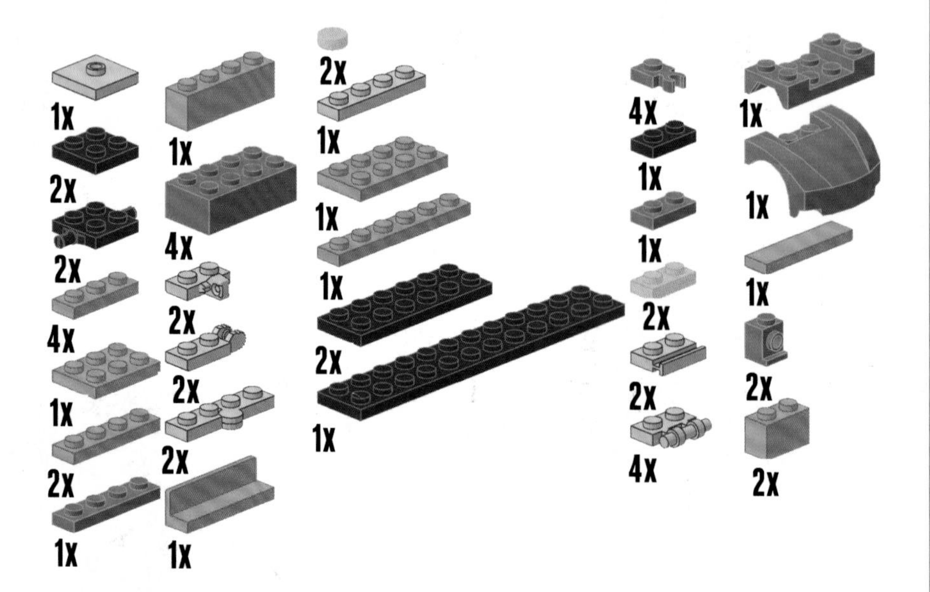

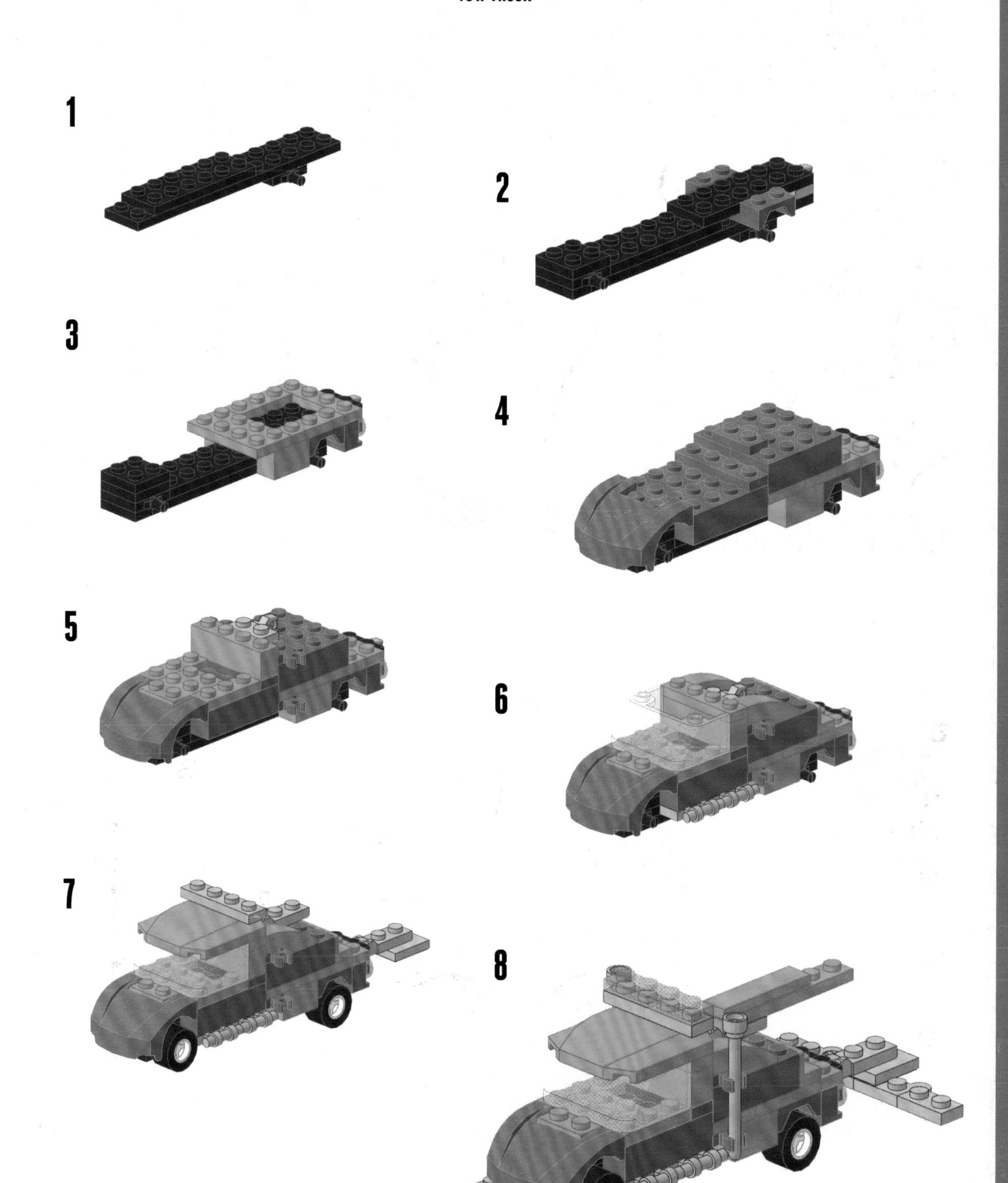
1
2
3
4
5
6
7
8

school bus

The big yellow school bus—an American icon—has been used to transport students to and from school for decades. Per the federal government, they are all painted the same eye-catching color and have specific safety and warning devices. LEGO®'s 1 x 4 yellow curved slope bricks are used for the roof and hood and give the bus its unmistakable shape. We've used several 1 x 1 plates in transparent red and orange to act as the warning lights.

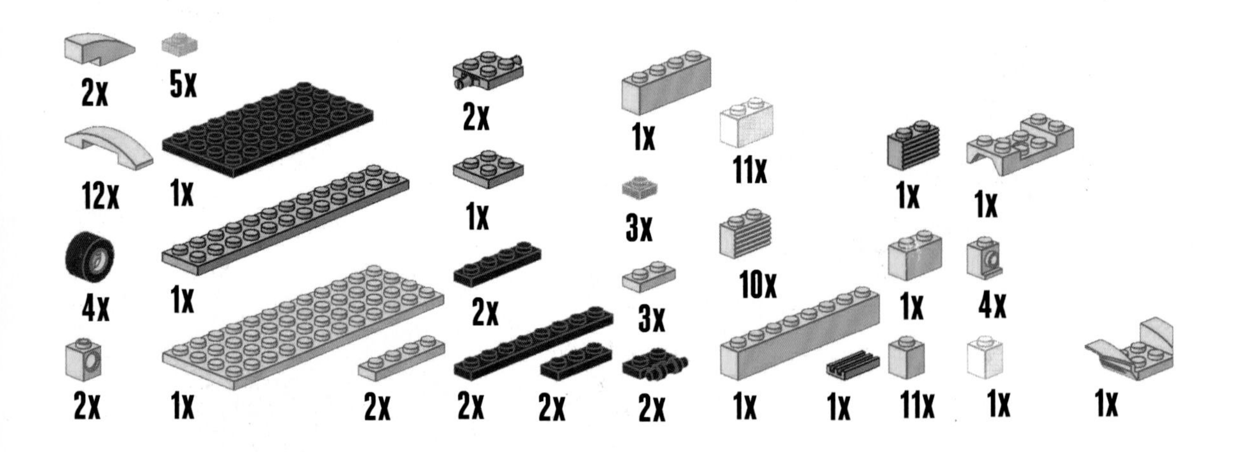

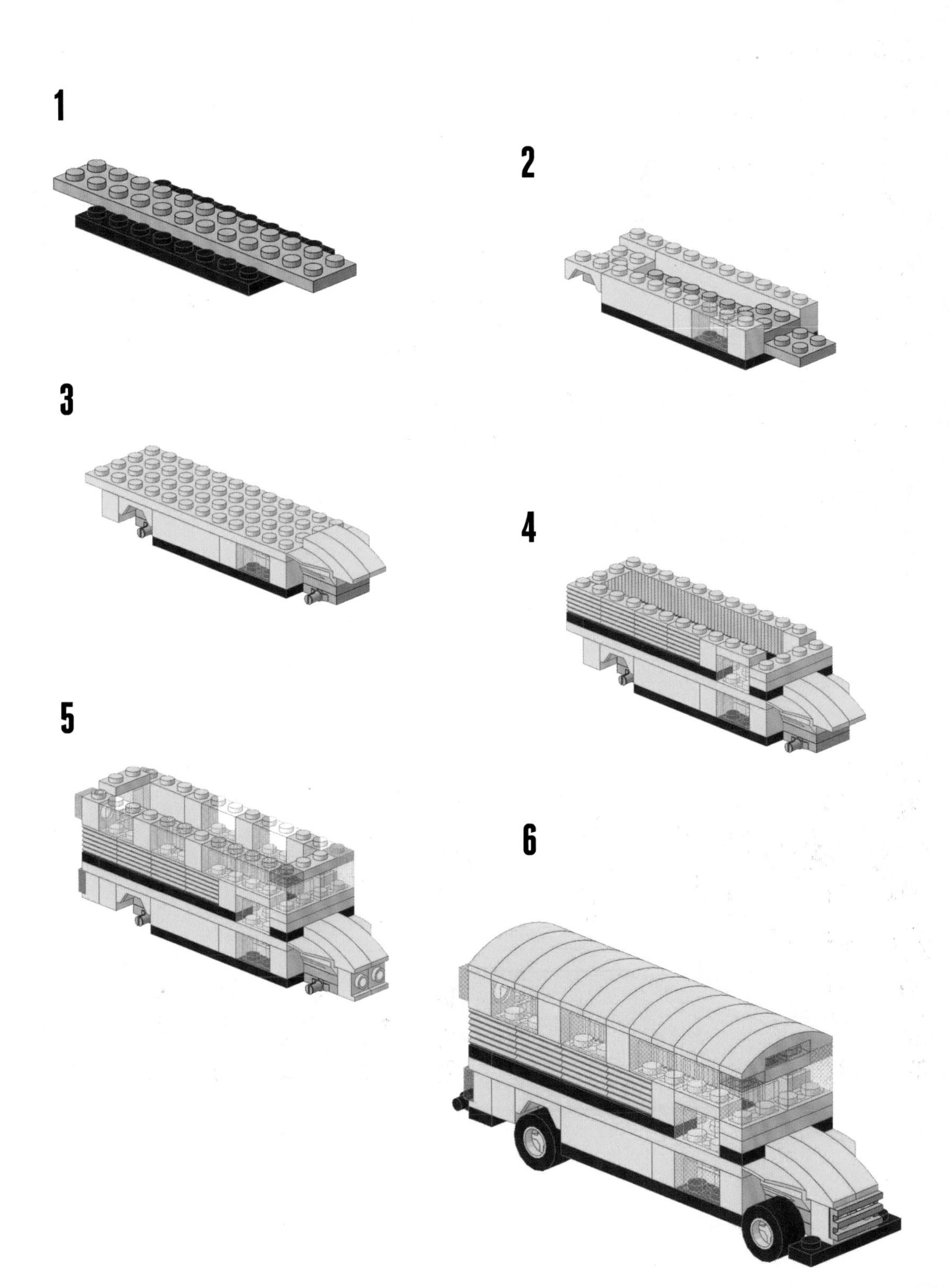
1
2
3
4
5
6

vw camper

An absolute classic, the VW camper van is recognized around the world. Synonymous with the hippie movement, Woodstock, and surfer culture, it's still popular today and remains a regular on the festival circuit. Vintage campers are sought after by collectors and road-trippers alike, especially those after a vacation on four wheels. Our bright orange camper has its signature spare tire on the front and a 1 × 2 profile brick for the radiator. 1 × 2 × 2 transparent panels are used to show off the abundance of windows, so the whole family gets a great view.

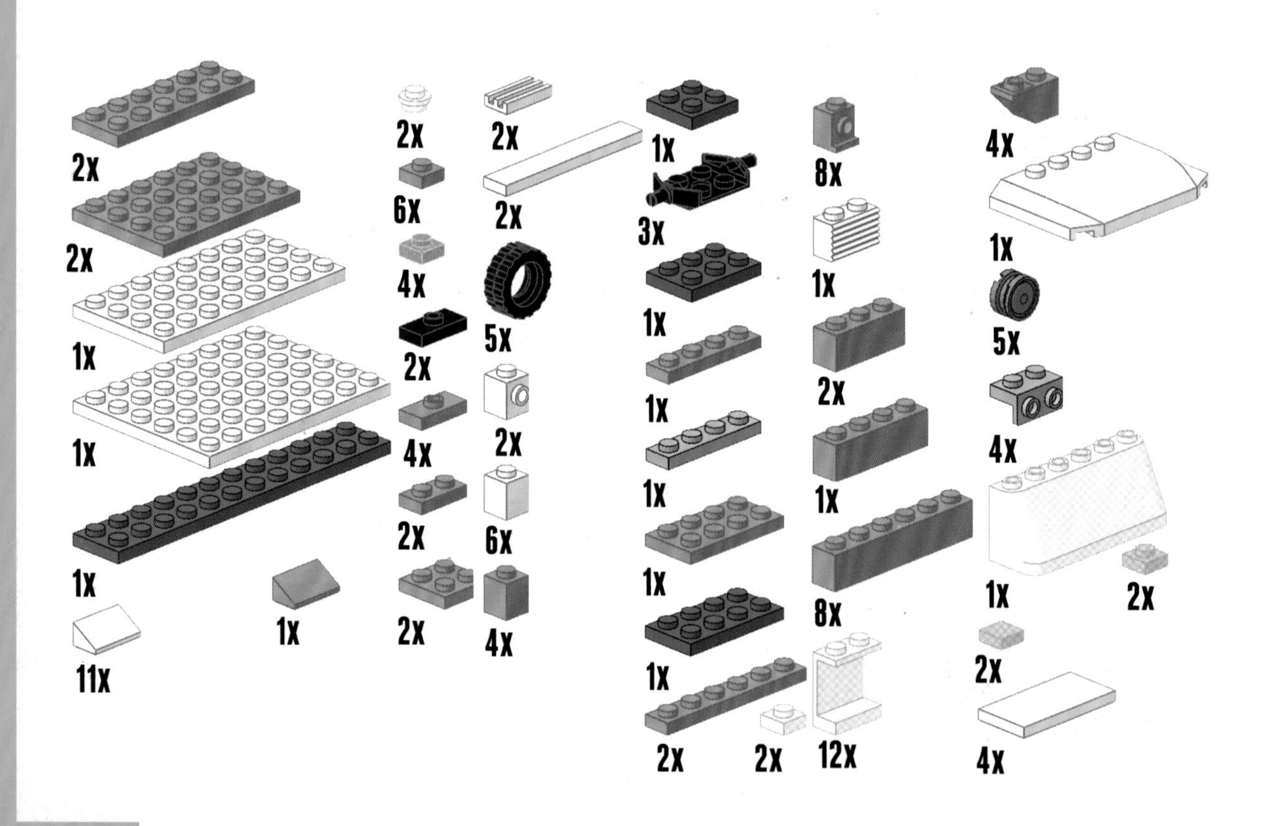

1

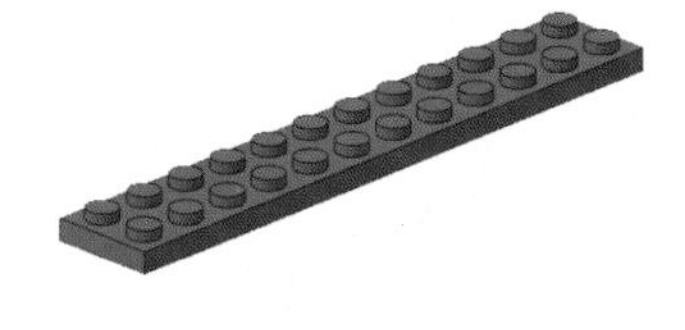

2

3

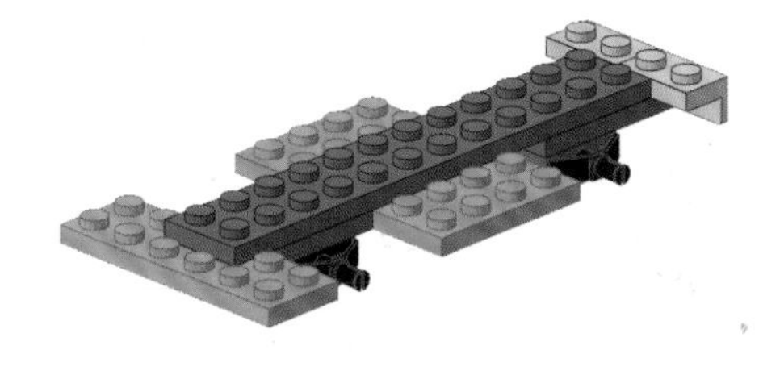

4

5

6

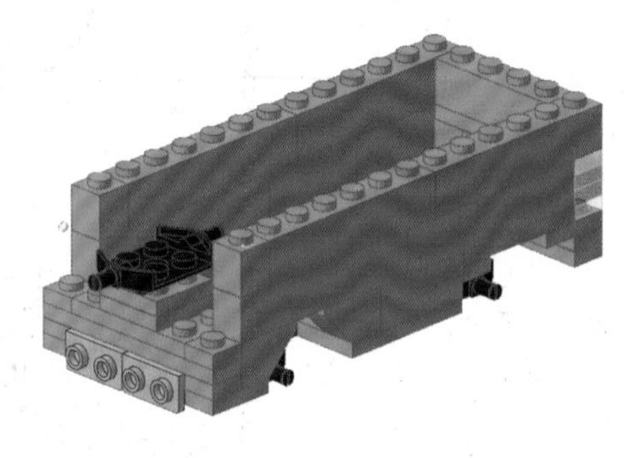

7

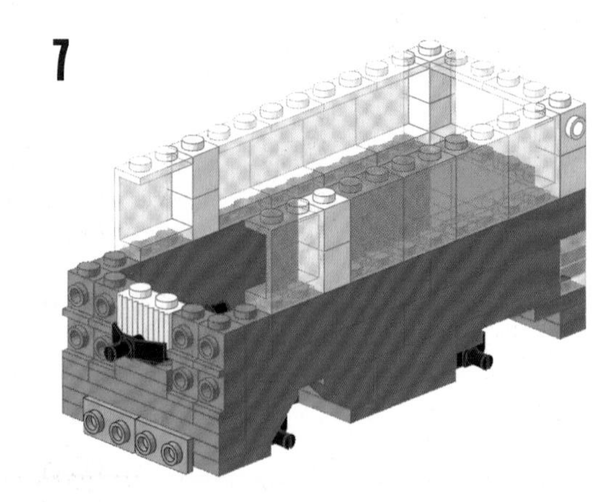

8

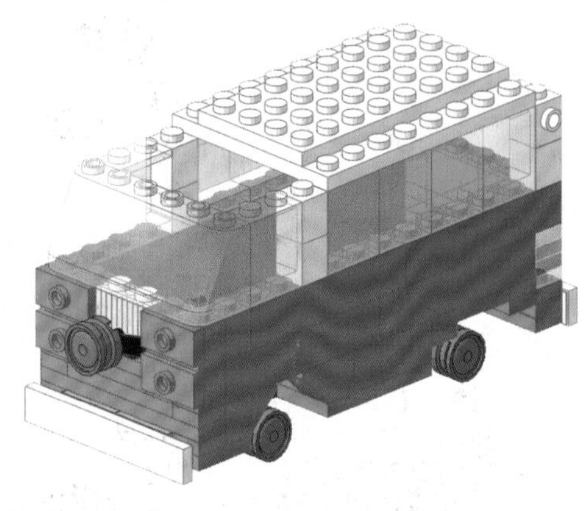

9

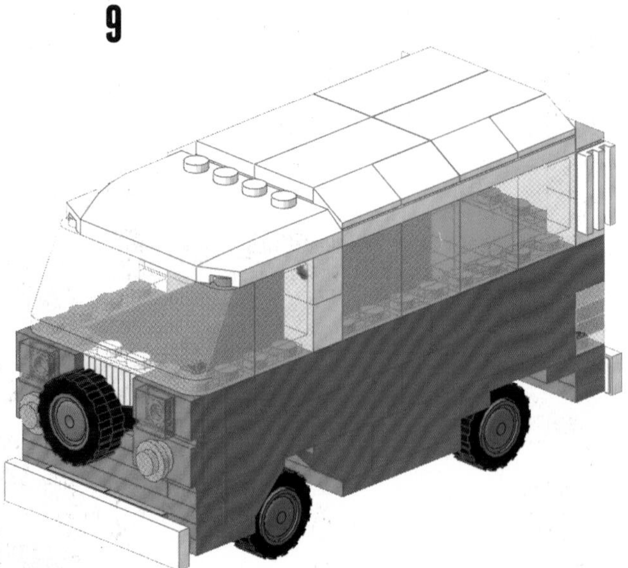

forklift

Seen in warehouses and shipyards the world over, the forklift was designed to lift and move heavy loads over short distances. Our forklift is battery-powered—check out the big battery strapped to the back, which helps to balance out the heavy loads carried on the metal forks at the front—recreated with LEGO®'s specially designed piece. Although widely available, it does not come in the CLASSIC kit. The indicator lights added to the upright bars are a safety must, warning that the forklift is zipping around.

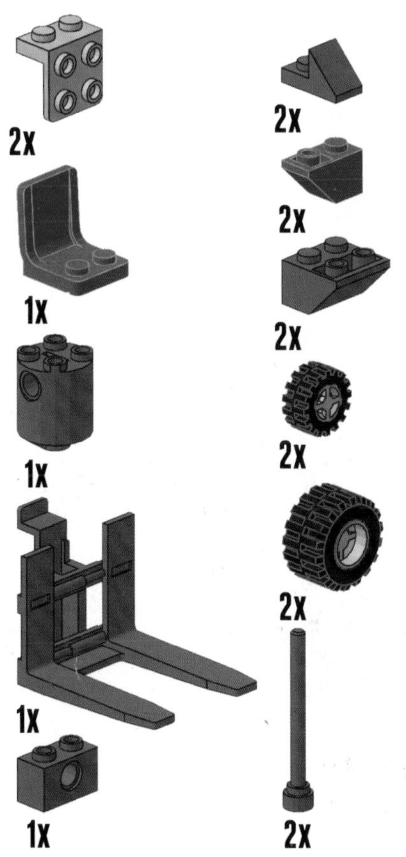

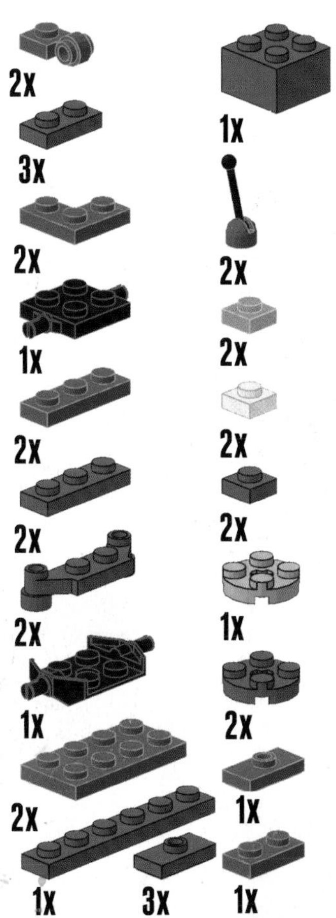

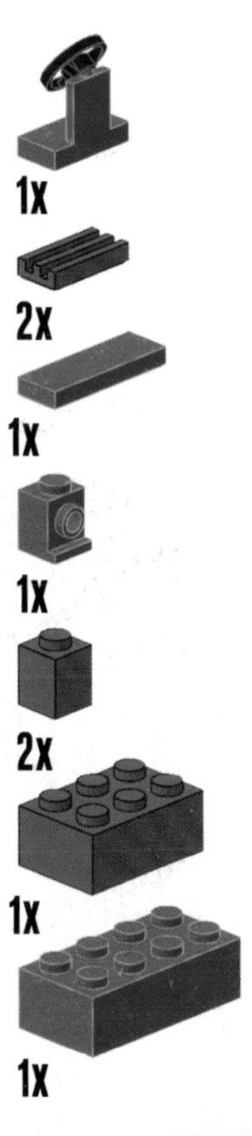

1

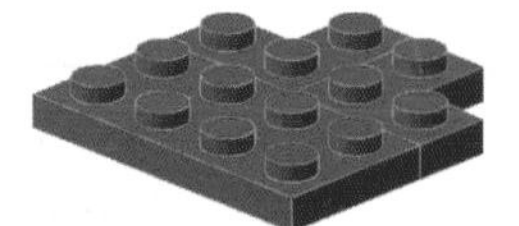

2

3

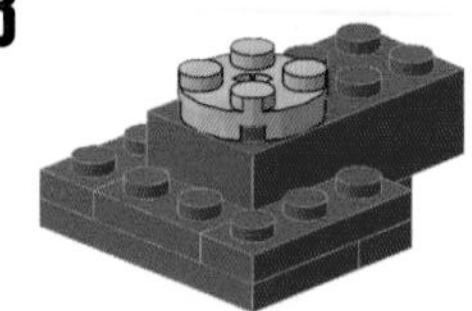

4

5

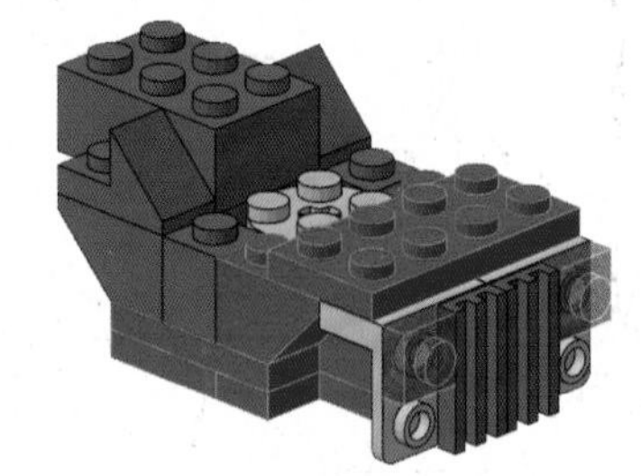

6

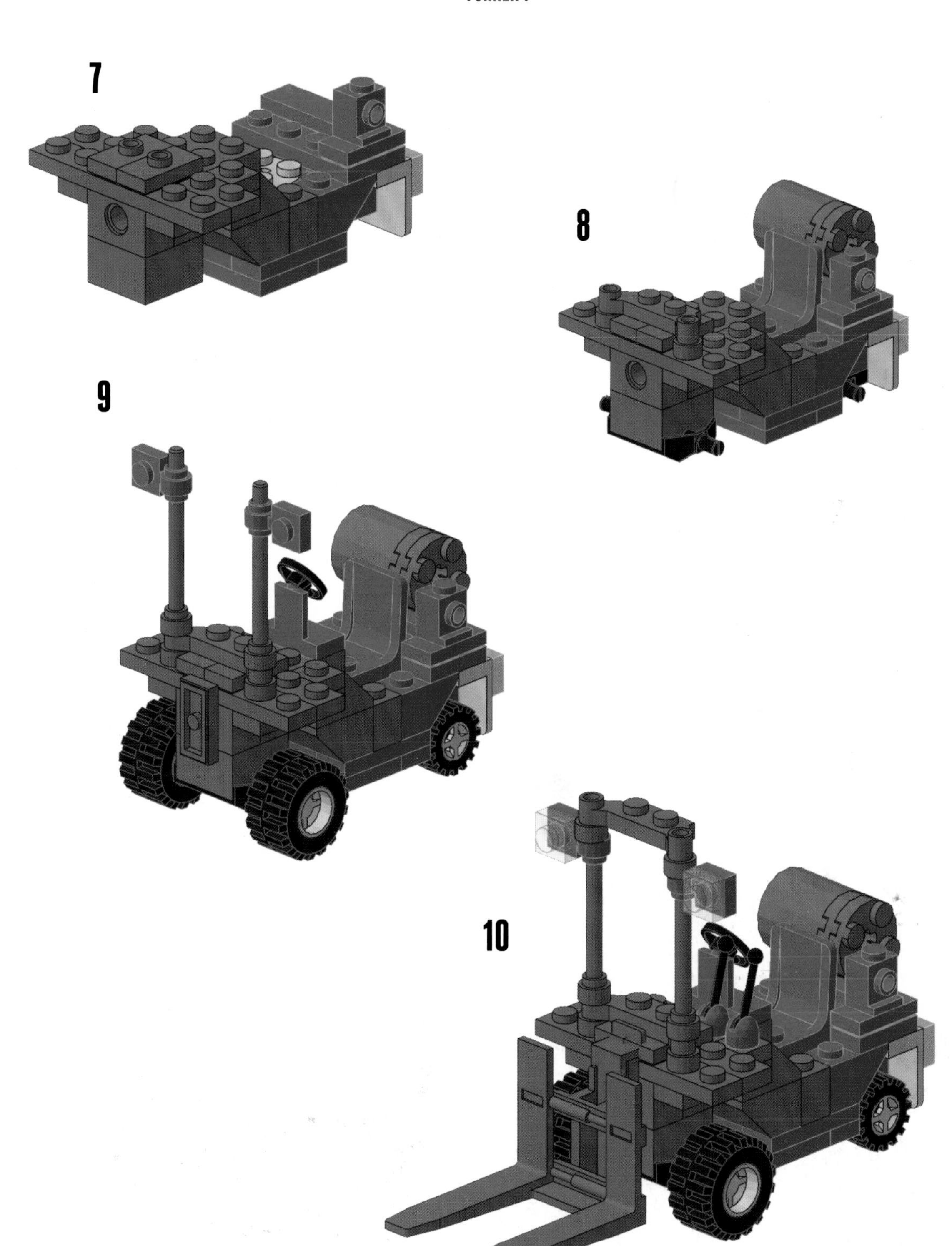
7
8
9
10

mobile crane

Our mobile crane is perfect for easily transporting a crane onto a site with minimal hassle. With little setup needed, these hydraulic-powered cranes—fitted with a telescopic boom and mounted on wheels—are ready to get to work as soon as they arrive. We've used a 1 x 1 x 5 column brick for the long arm and a 1 x 2 transparent brick for the operator's cab. The crane has four axles in two pairs and 1 x 2, 45-degree slopes for the outriggers. These are used to keep the crane stable before the operator lifts the boom arm.

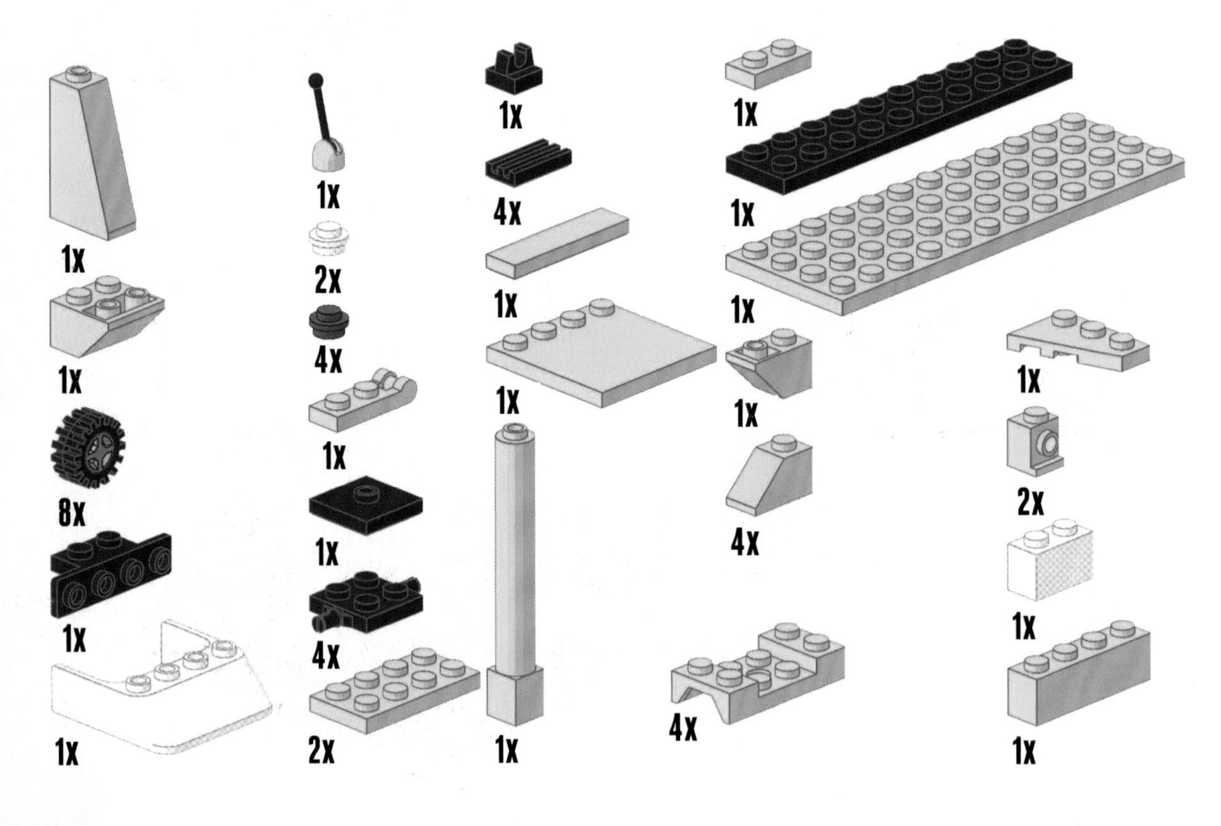

1

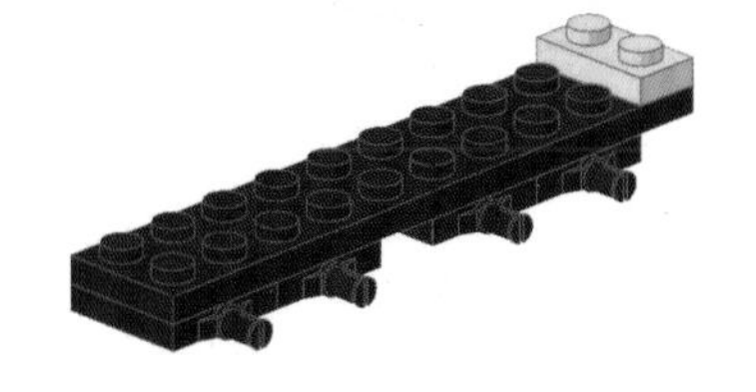

2

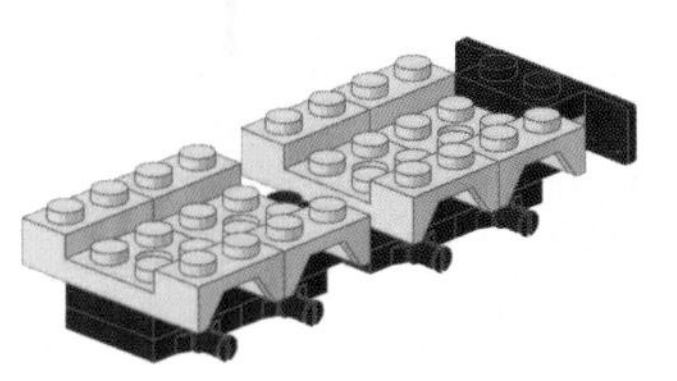

3

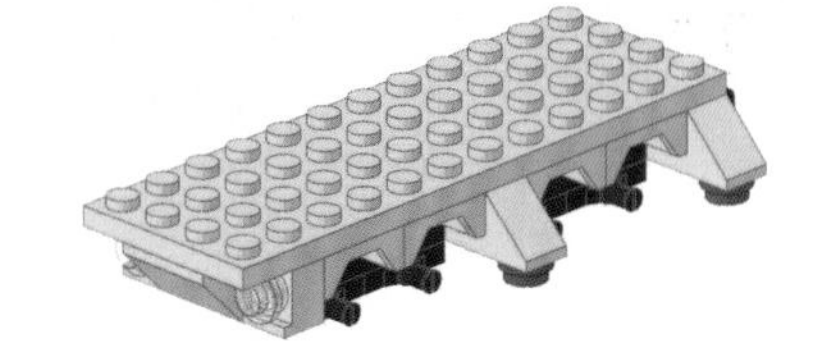

4

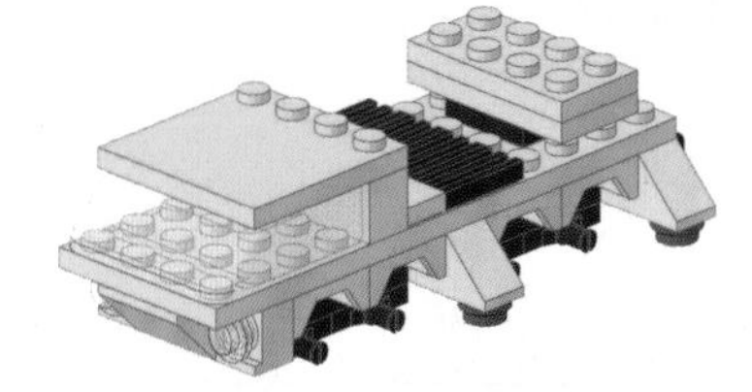

5

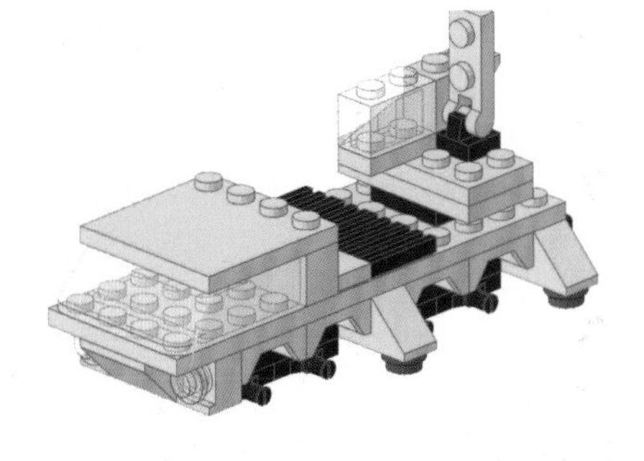

6

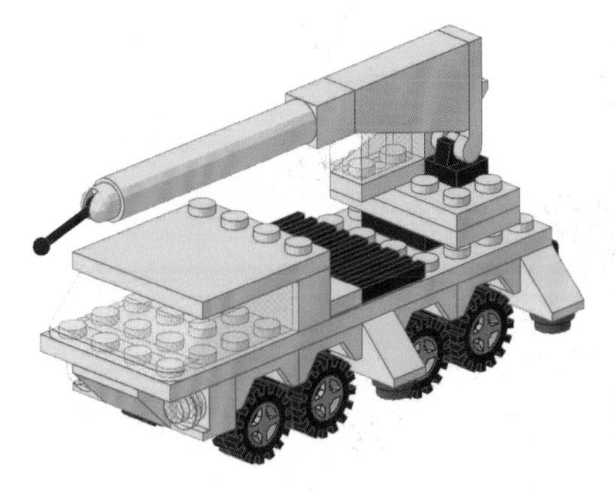

sports car

If you want a powerful, lightweight set of wheels—with agile handling and speedy performance—get yourself a sports car! They can be filled with every luxury or stripped right back to basics, but are usually low-slung and flashy, with aerodynamic body kits to boost their road-handling. 2 x 2, 45-degree transparent slopes make up the windshield of this one, while the small curved slopes of the hood and trunk make out its sleek styling. The swooped curve is finished off with a convex curve to create the spoiler.

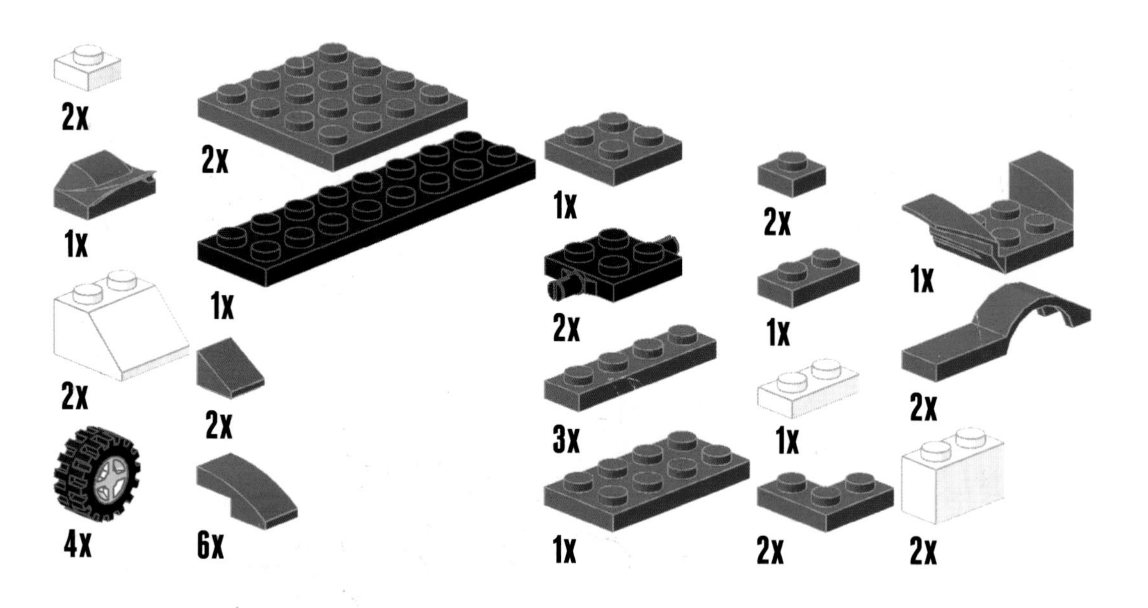

1

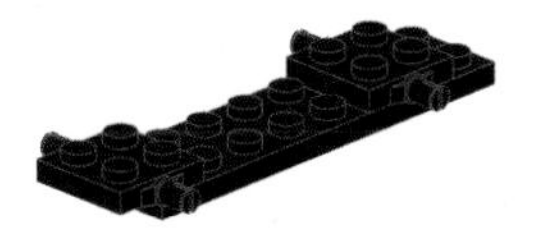

2

3

4

5

6

7

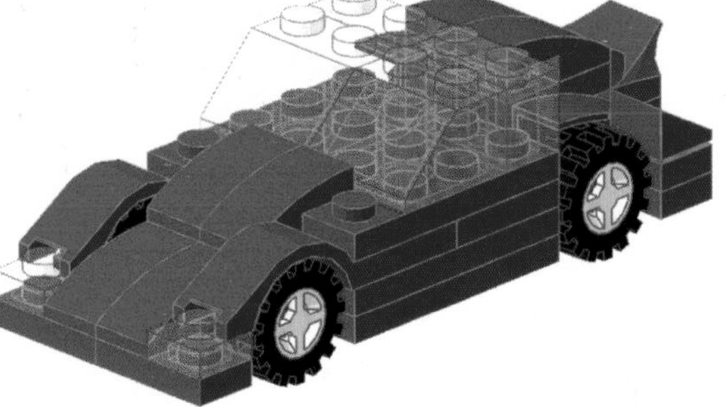

digger

The digger, or JCB®, is the king of the construction site. When a shovel just won't cut it, they're brought in to dig huge holes. Created by, and named after the company's founder, Joseph Cyril Bamford, they have been shoveling dirt since 1948. Our JCB is bright yellow, just like all the machines produced by JCB since 1951. While there are more than 150 models, we've chosen to recreate a combination backhoe and loader. The bucket at the front is created by using two upturned chair pieces. In the United States, the similar Bobcat® is a familiar sight in its white and orange colors.

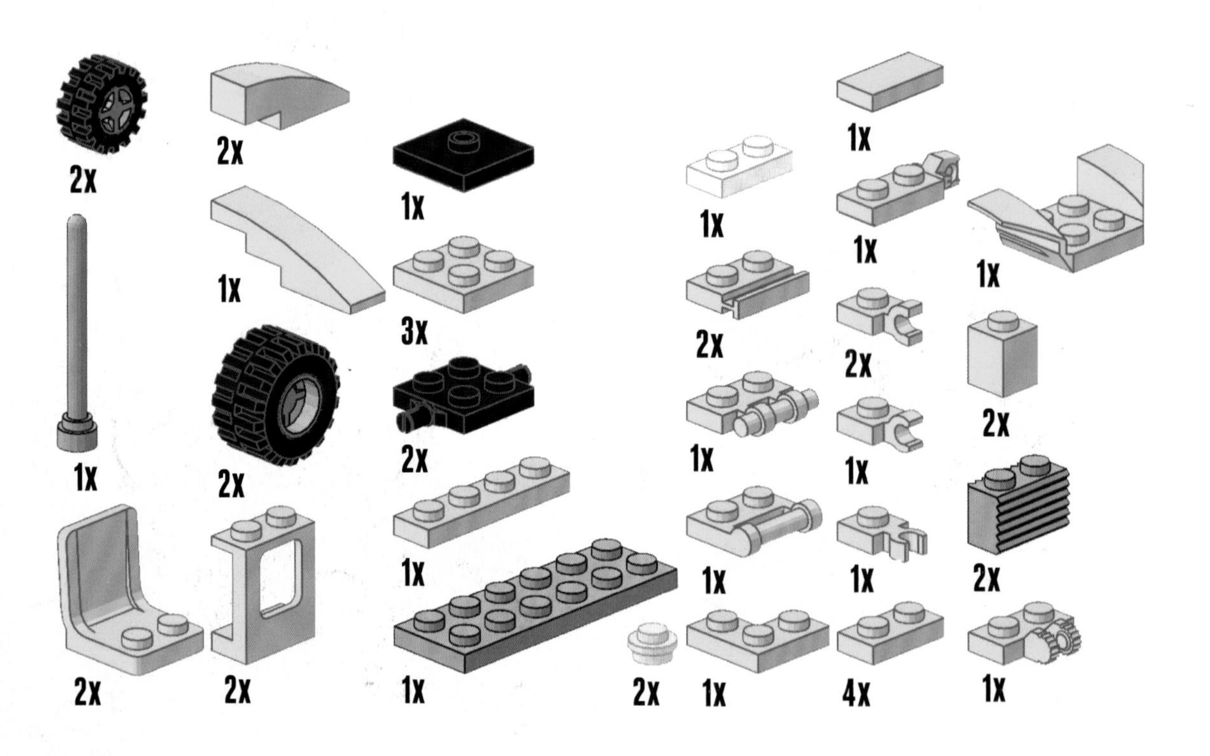

1

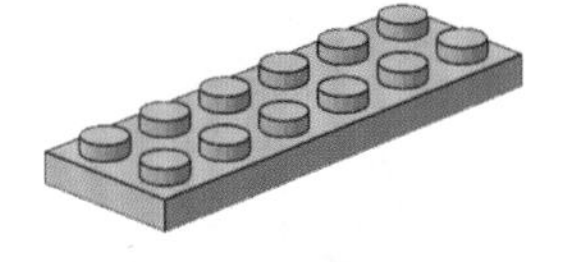

2

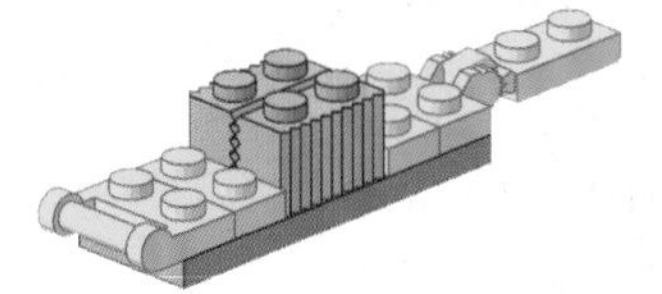

3

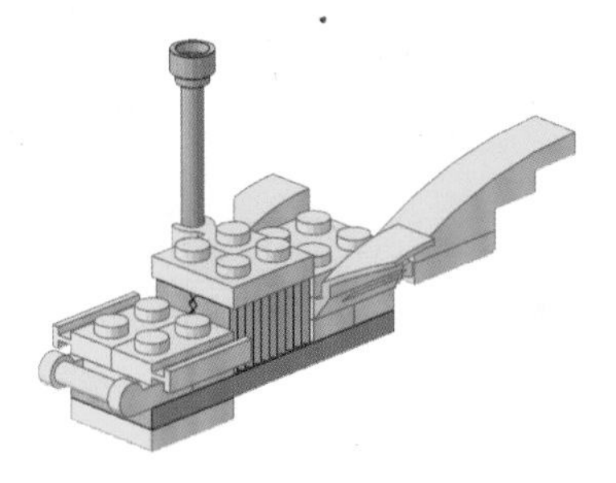

4

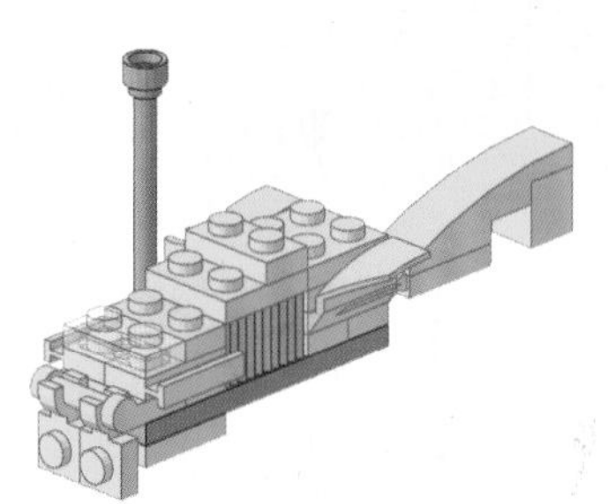

5

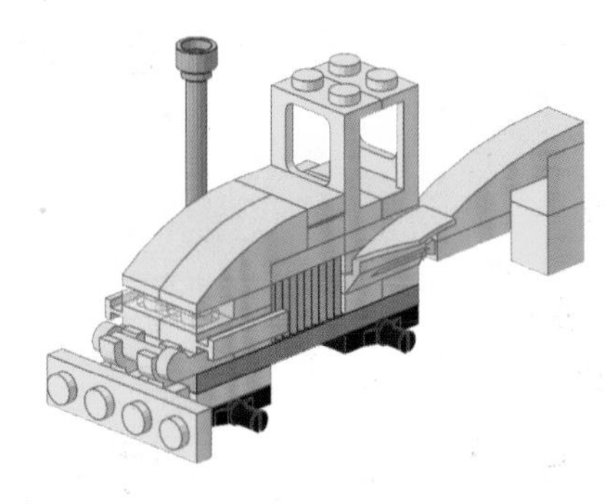

6

snowplow

Snow is falling all around me. It's time to call out the snowplow! Specially adapted to clear snow from the streets during heavy winter storms, the snowplow is often combined with a grit spreader to stop them from icing over. The undercarriage sides have been created by attaching 1 x 4 curved slopes to the body. The shovel itself is made from 2 x 4 wedge plates mounted on a bracket. Large overhead lights have been set above the cab to warn other traffic that the snowplow is on its way.

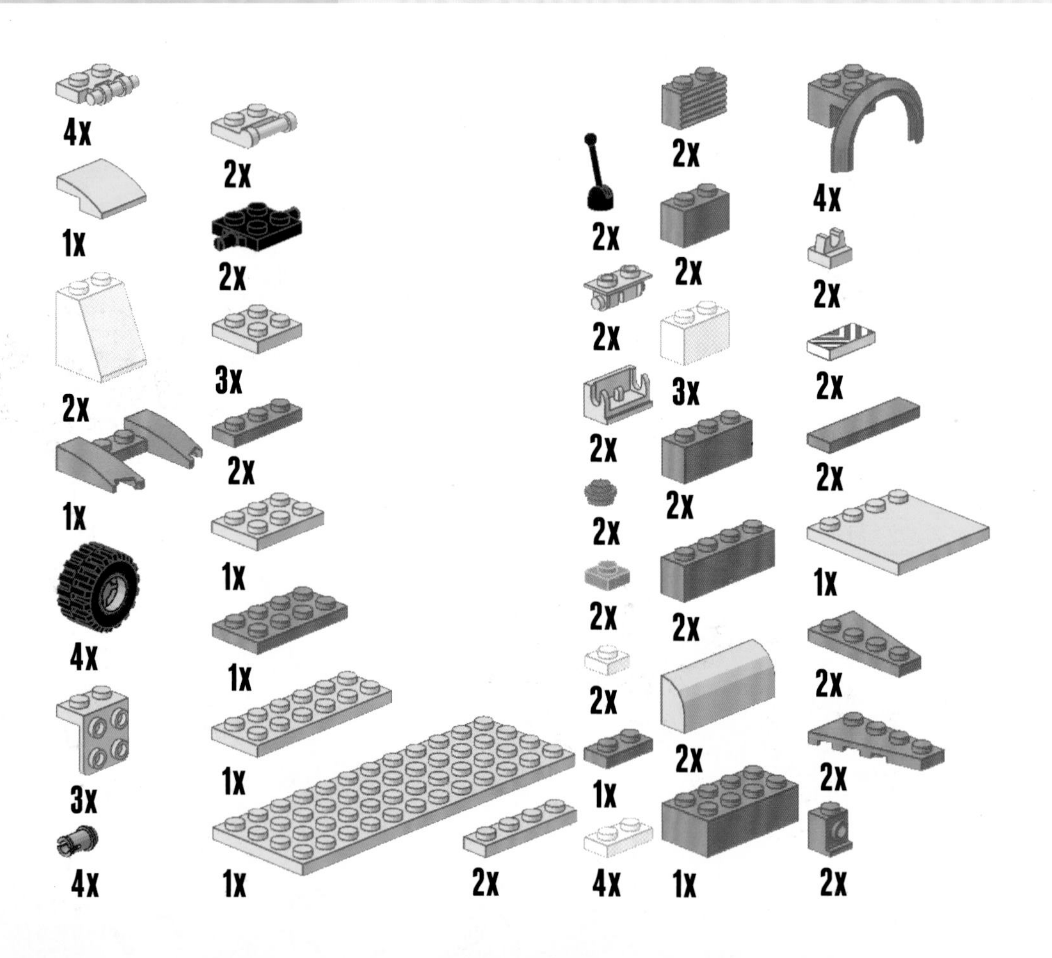

1

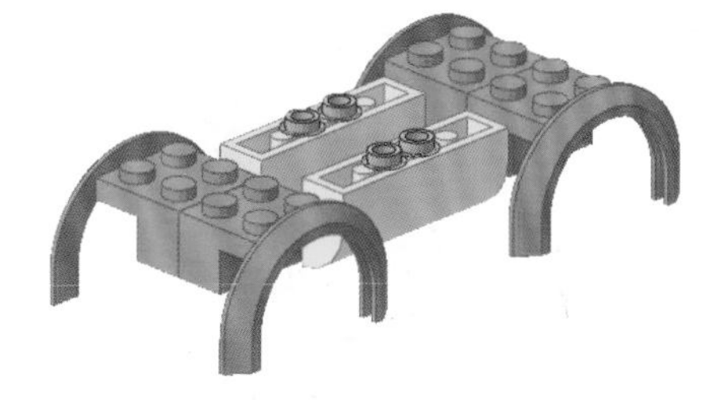

2

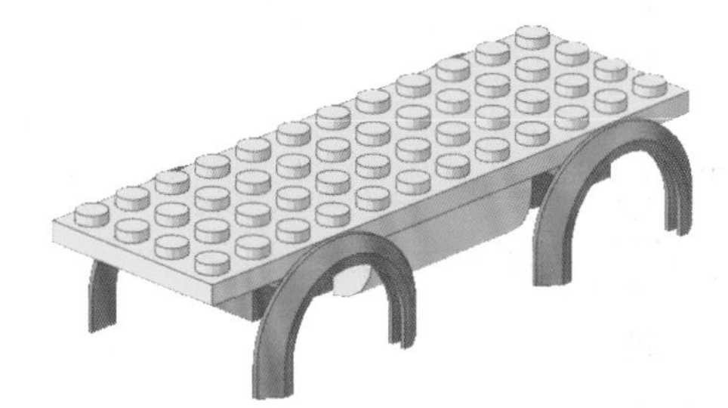

3

4

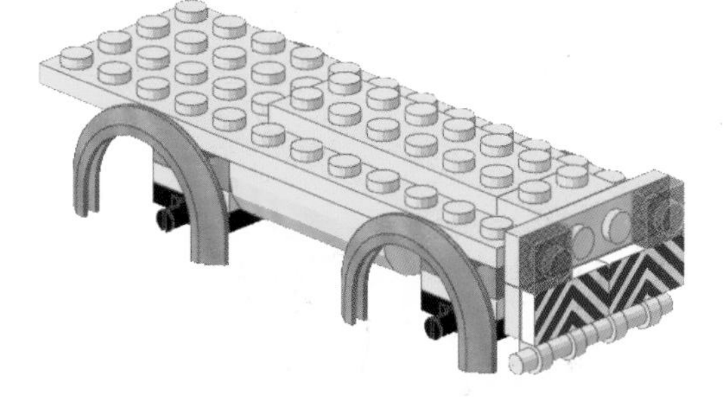

5

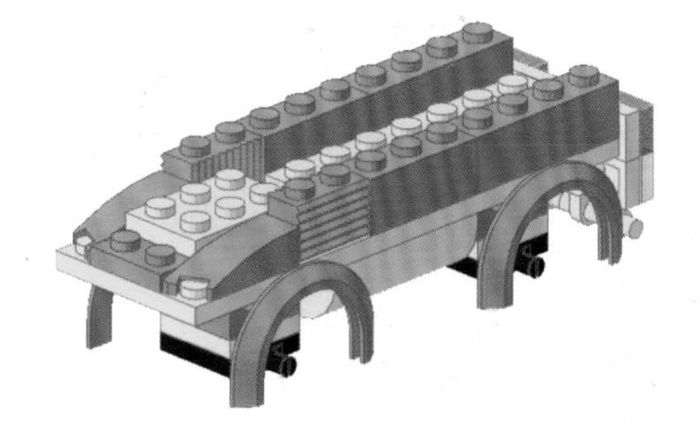

6

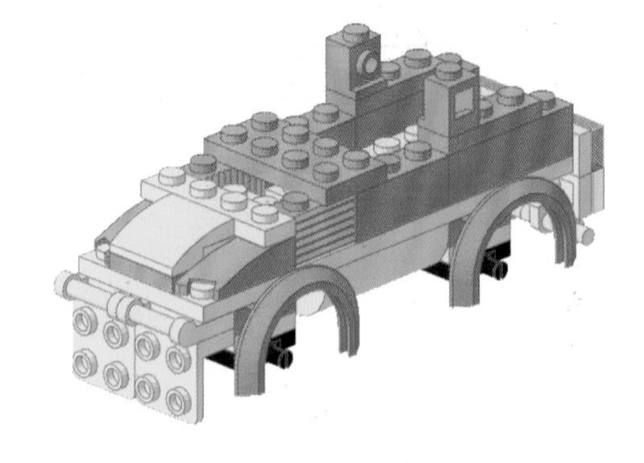

7

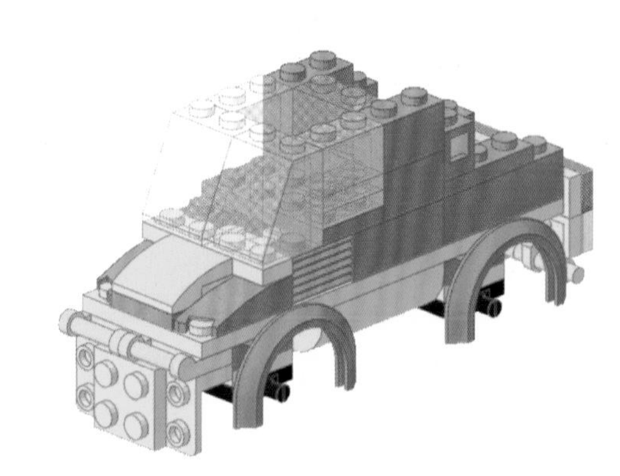

8

9

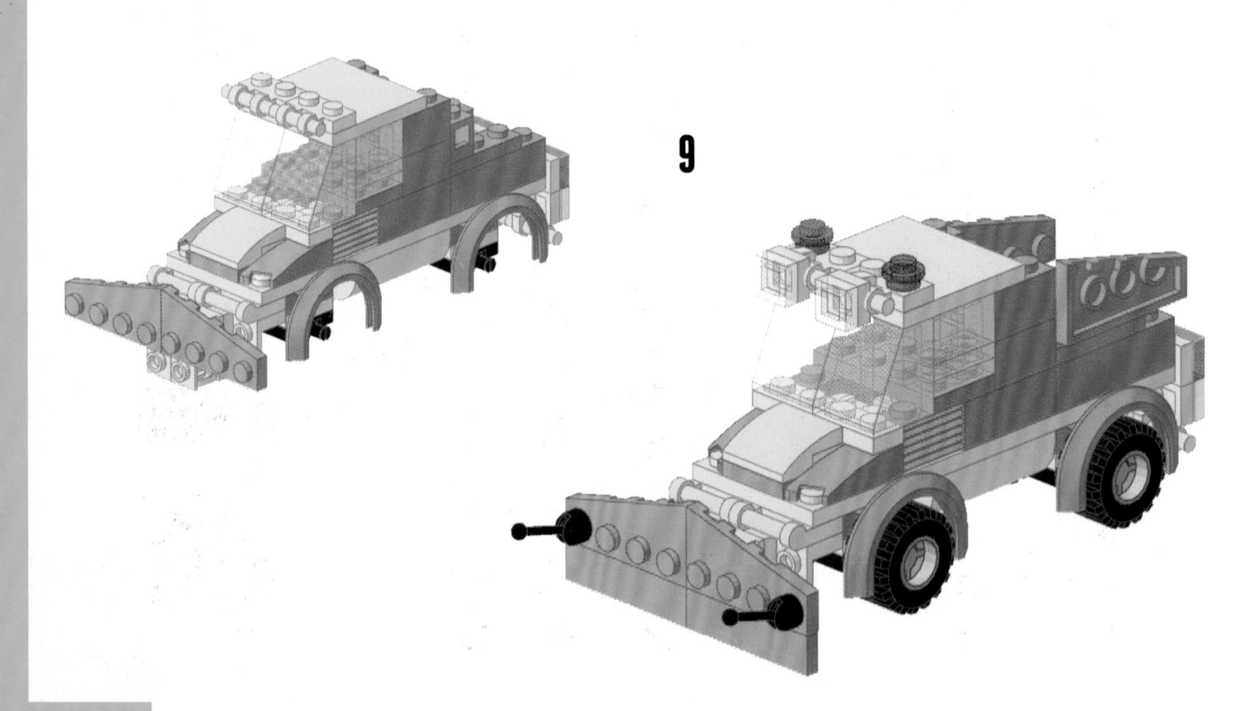

cement mixer

A cement mixer is instantly recognizable by the big twirling barrel fitted to its back. It is designed to transport bulk loads of cement to construction sites, mixing as it goes so the cement doesn't harden. We've recreated the drum shape of the mixer and fitted it to the base of our yellow truck. Its fat tires are perfect for driving around muddy sites. Two 1 x 2 cheese slopes, a 1 x 1 plate with clip, and a 1 x 2 plate with bar are used to create the exit chute for the cement at the back.

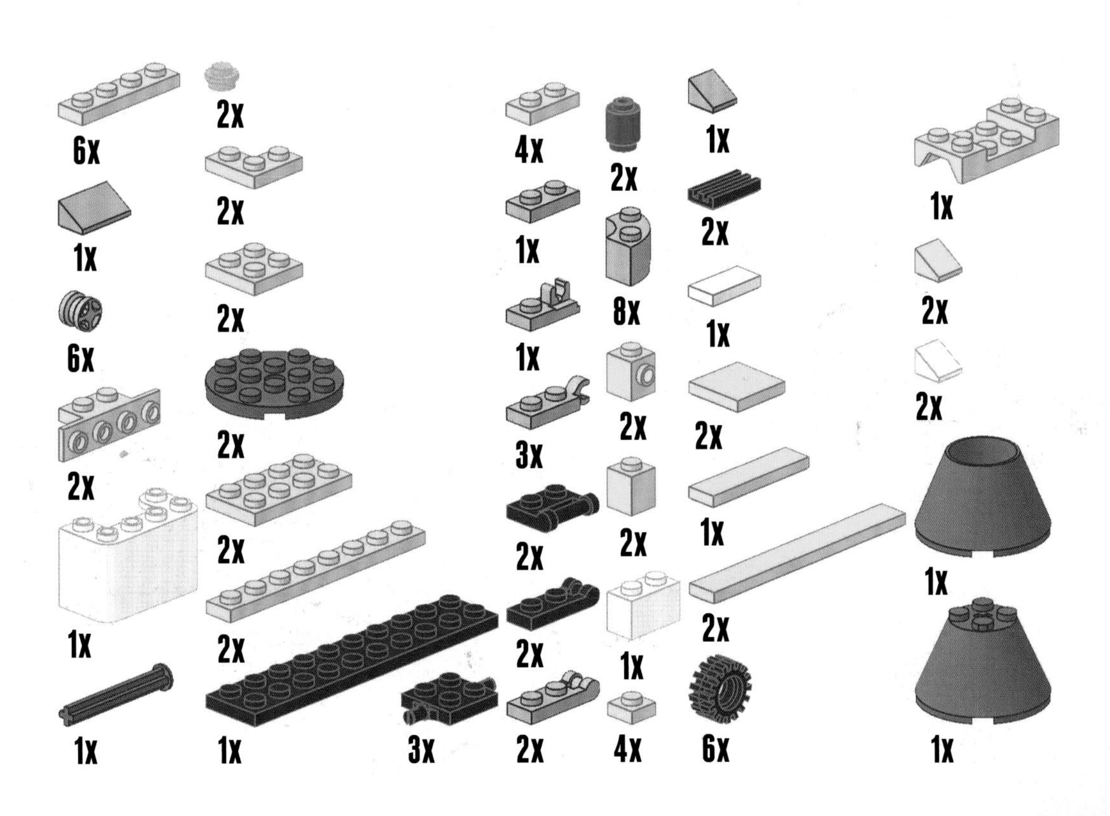

1

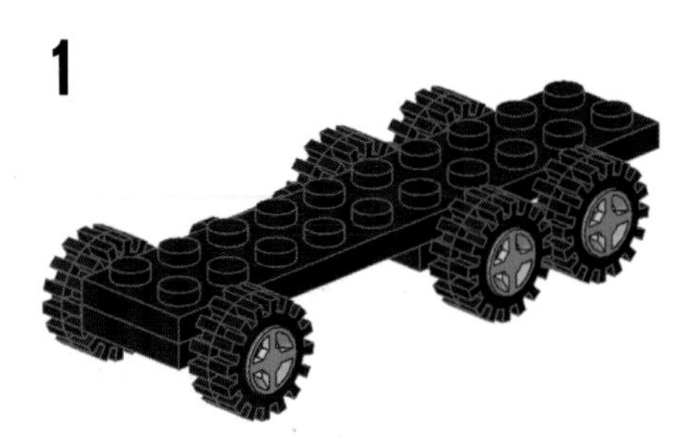

2

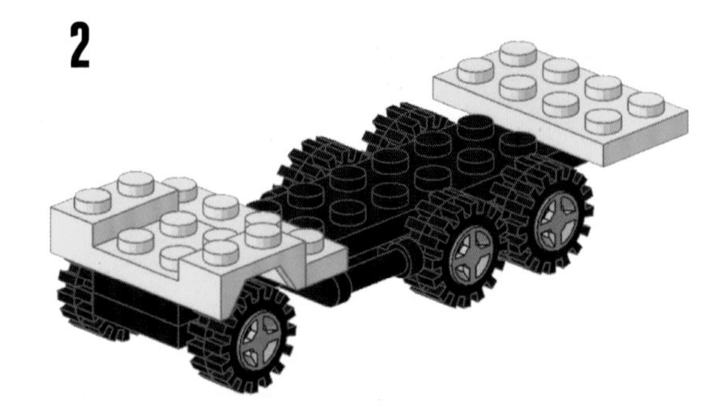

3

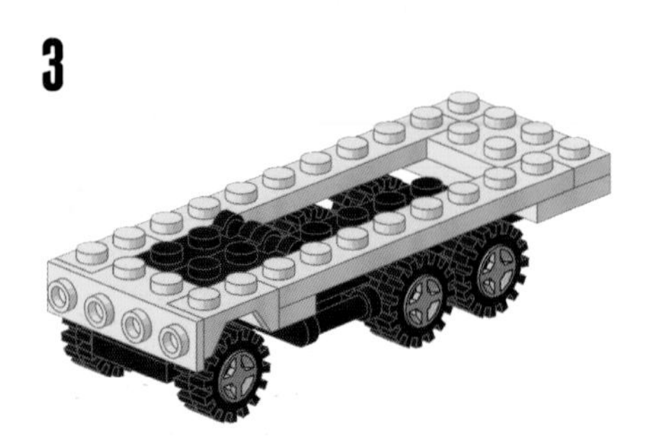

4

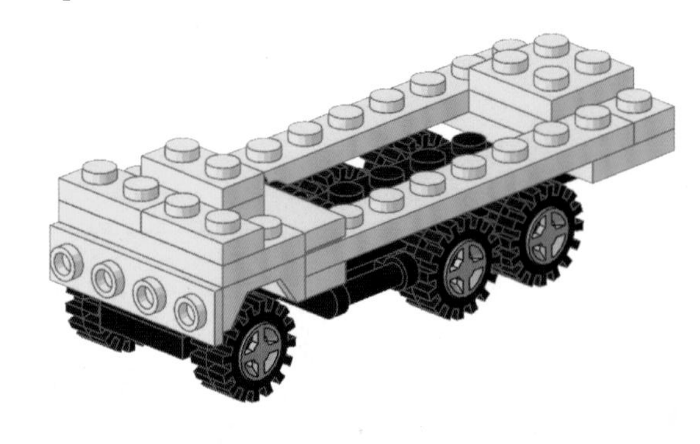

5

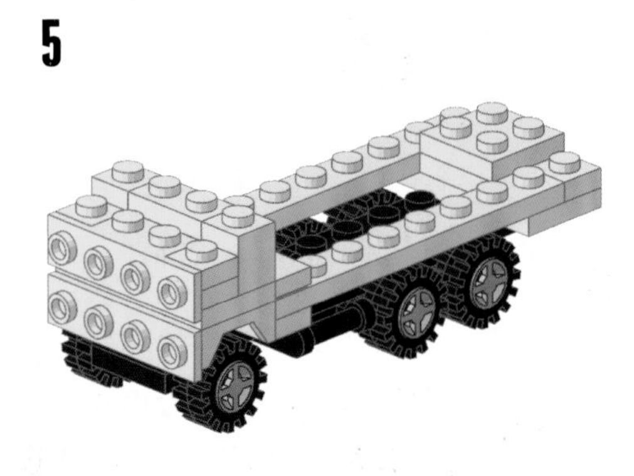

6

7

8

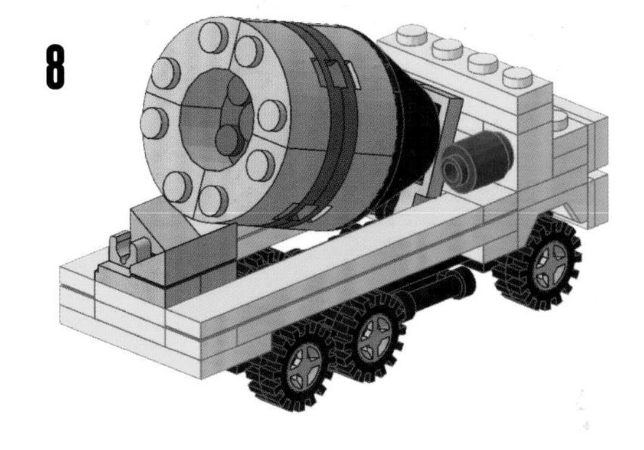

9

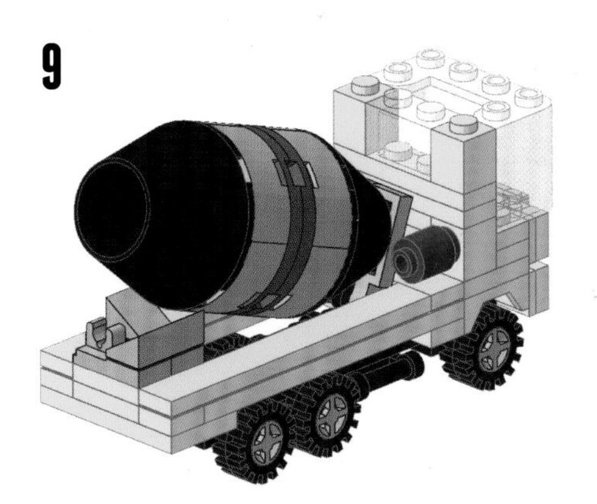

10

11

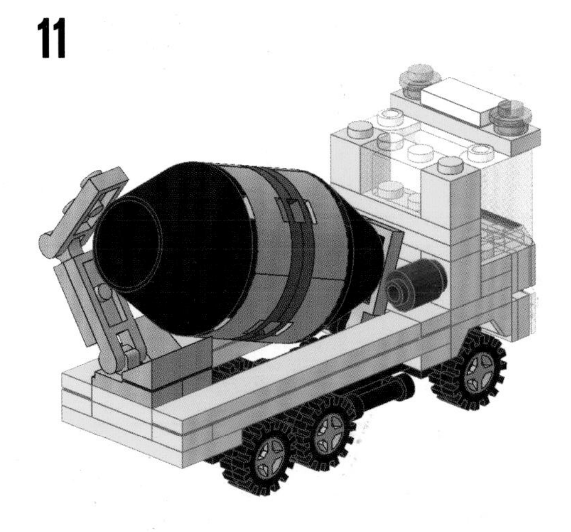

12

fire engine

We'd be in big trouble without fire engines, which are specially equipped with a ladder and hoses to fight fires and save lives. LEGO® red is a great match for fire-engine red. We've made this one in micro scale to show how you can use 1 x 2 plates with two clips as axle holders for the wheels. As well as carrying all the equipment needed for firefighters to put out fires, fire engines also have loud sirens and flashing lights to clear the way when speeding to an emergency. Our transparent blue bricks do the job nicely.

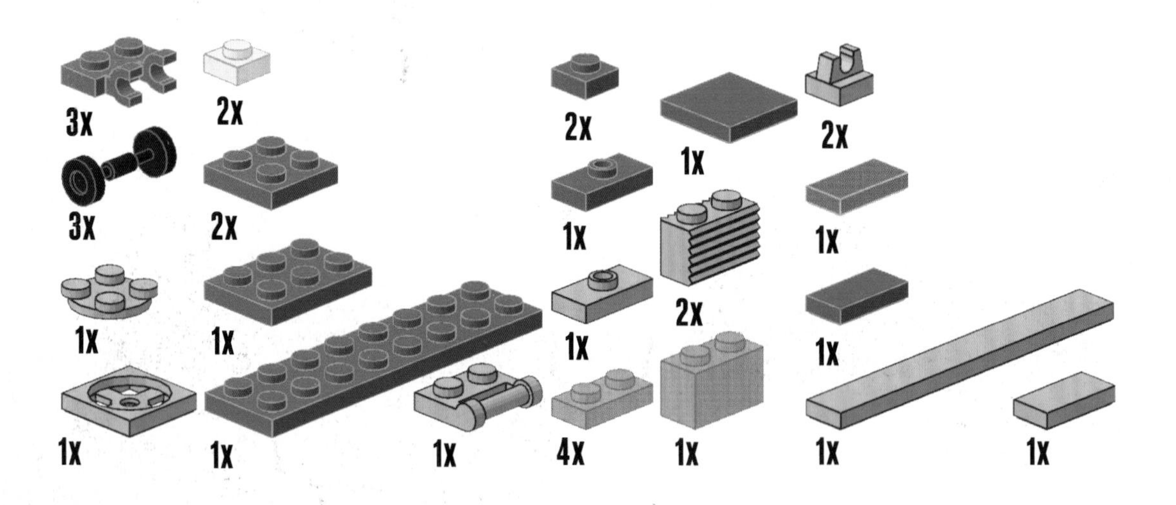

1

2

3

4

5

6

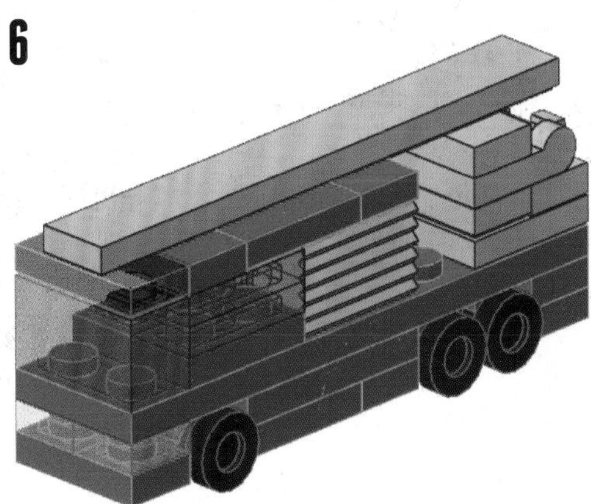

police car

Police cars are as varied as the towns and countries they police. In Dubai they are often simply converted sports cars, chosen for their speed! However, they all share a few standard fittings, such as sirens and flashing lights, and are decorated with the badge of their particular police force. The small wheels-and-axle part gives us a great start for this micro-scale police car, while combining the white and blue plates gives us the signature stripe around the middle of the bodywork of this cruiser. 1 × 2 transparent red, blue, and yellow plates make great lights.

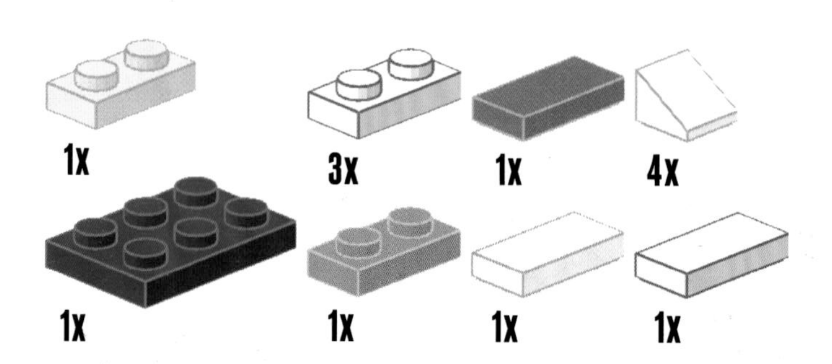

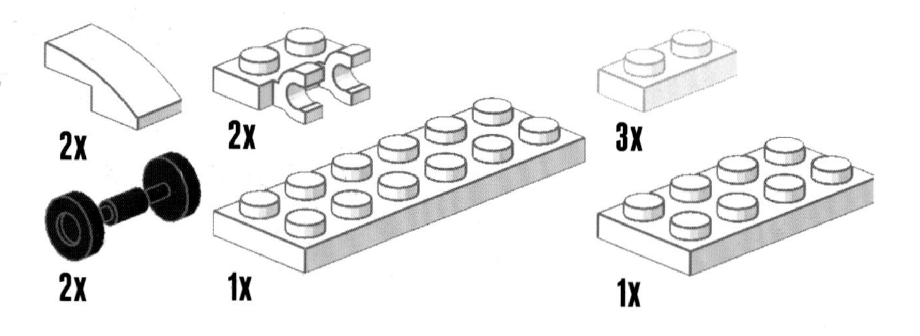

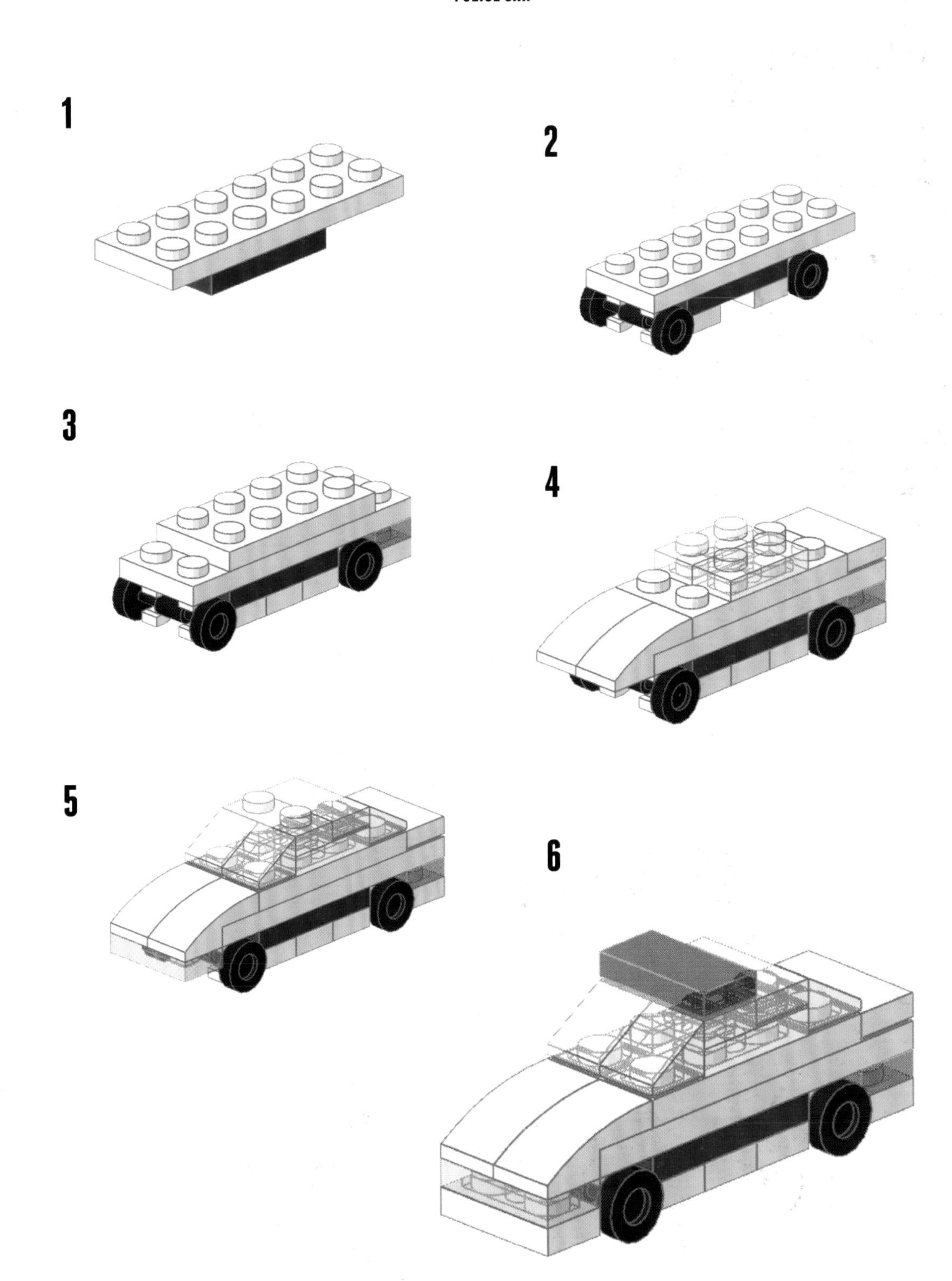
1
2
3
4
5
6

race car

You won't find many vehicles faster than a Formula 1 race car. They are the ultimate driving machine! They are light, with a single bucket seat, an open cockpit, and large wings. The engine is positioned behind the driver. Their design is sleek, low-slung, and aerodynamic, allowing them to speed around the track at more than 300 kmph (185 mph). For our micro-scale model we've used 1 x 1 plates with a lamp-holder to hold together the two sides of the blue driver's seating area. The small curved slopes on each side give us the car's characteristic shape.

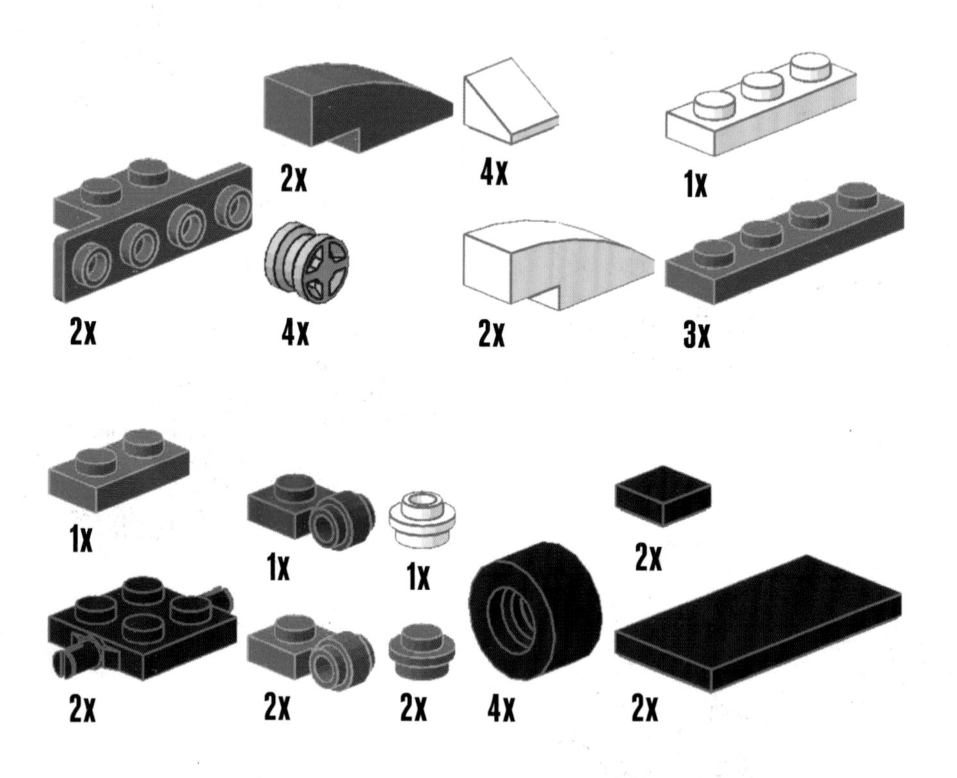

1

2

3

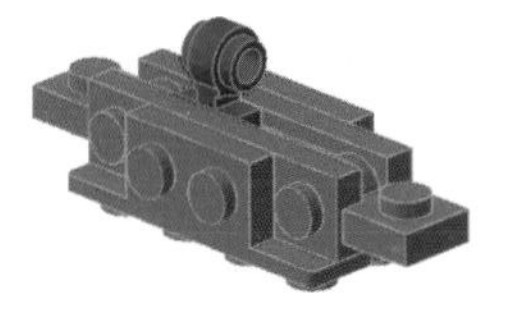

4

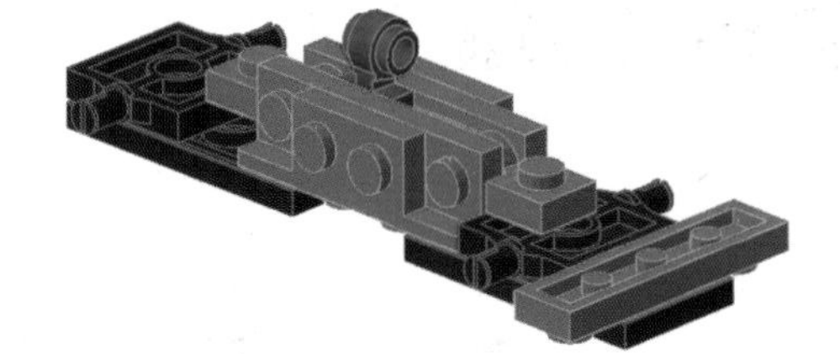

5

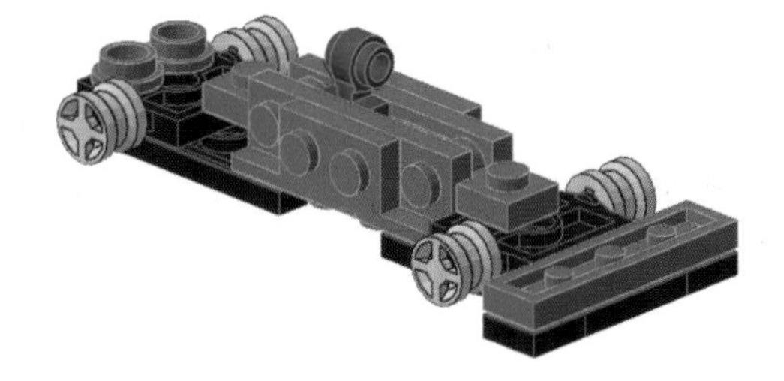

6

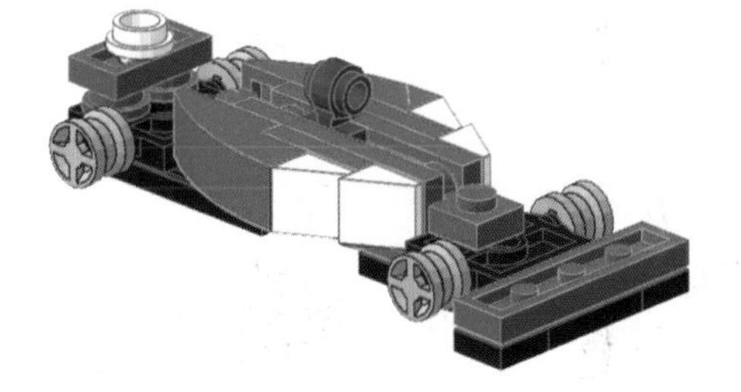

7

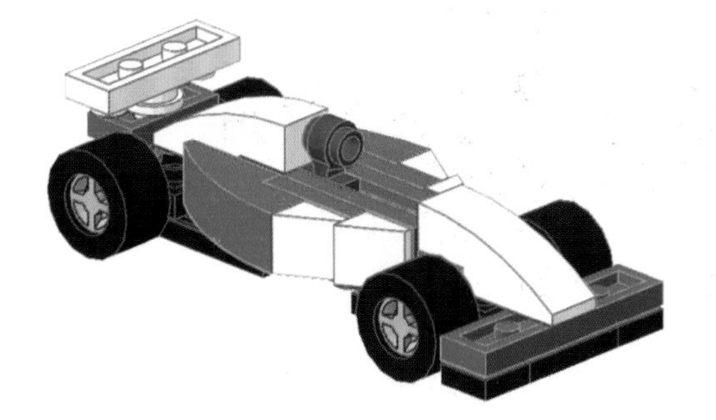

car carrier

A car carrier is a specially designed trailer built to transport several cars or vans at once, often when they're fresh from the factory. They typically have two or three tiers, each carrying up to five cars. The front of the top tier usually overhangs the top of the truck cab, while a ramp at the back of the carrier allows the cars to be loaded and unloaded. We've created the simplest micro-scale depiction of cars for our model—seven in total!

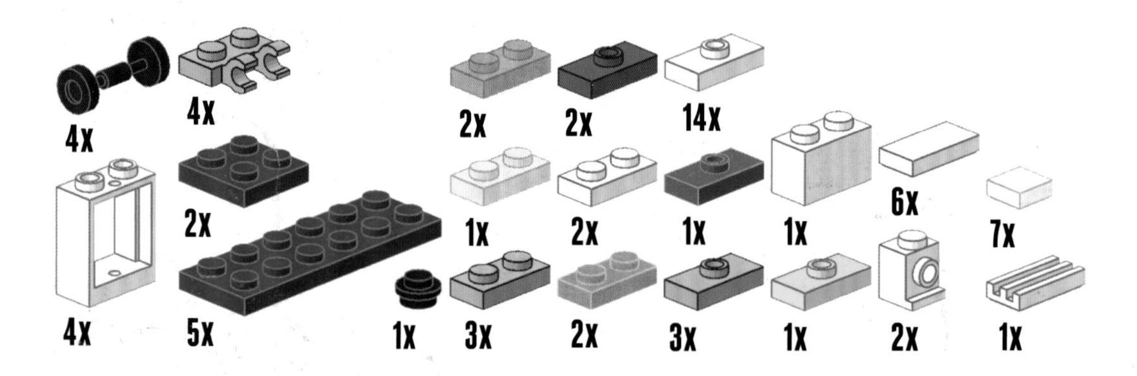

1

2

3

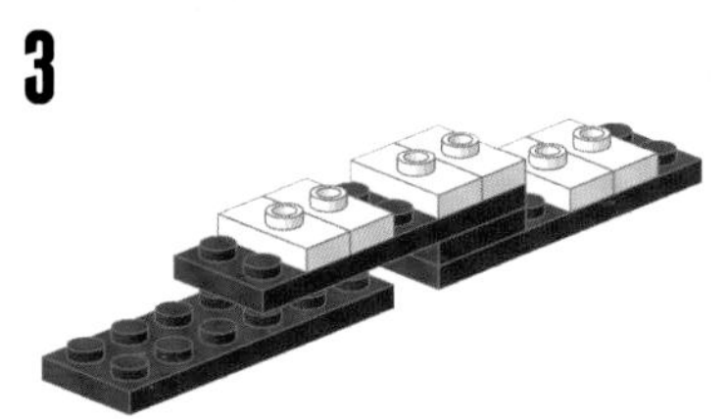

4

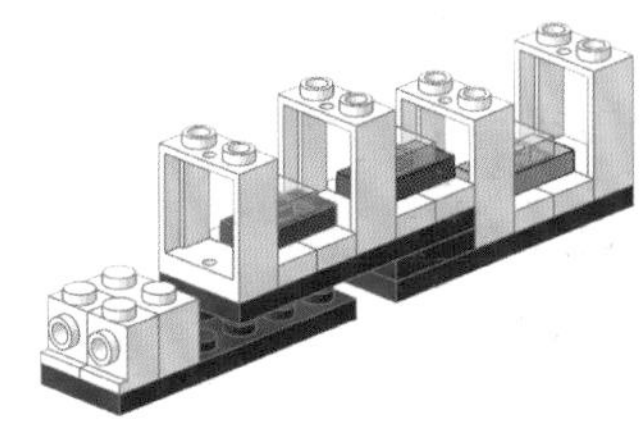

5

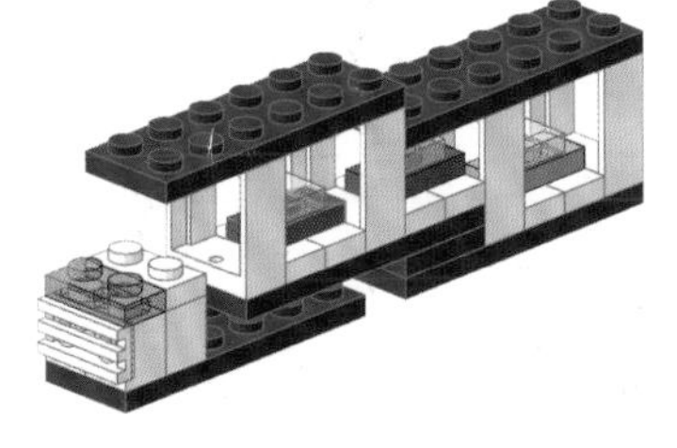

6

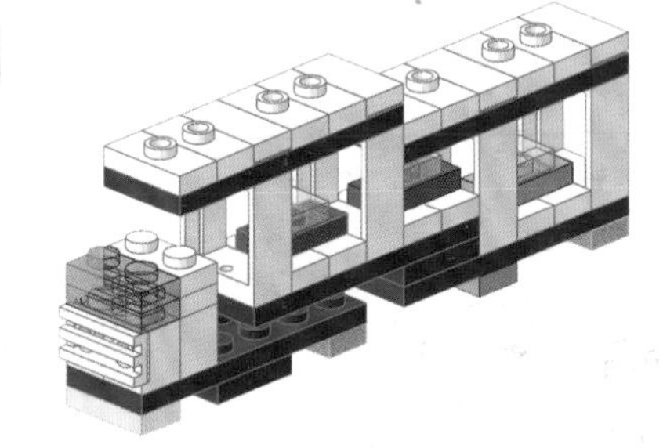

7

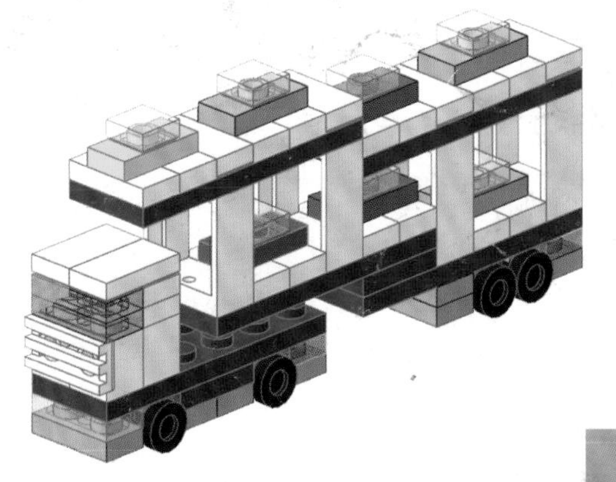

quad bike

The quad bike is the adrenaline junkie's dream! Designed as an all-terrain vehicle, its low-pressure tires mean it can speed through mud, across streams, and up hills. Similar to a motorbike, the driver straddles the seat, using handlebars to steer and control speed. But the extra wheels give it more stability at slower speeds. Although usually equipped with three or four wheels, you can get six-wheel models for specialized functions.

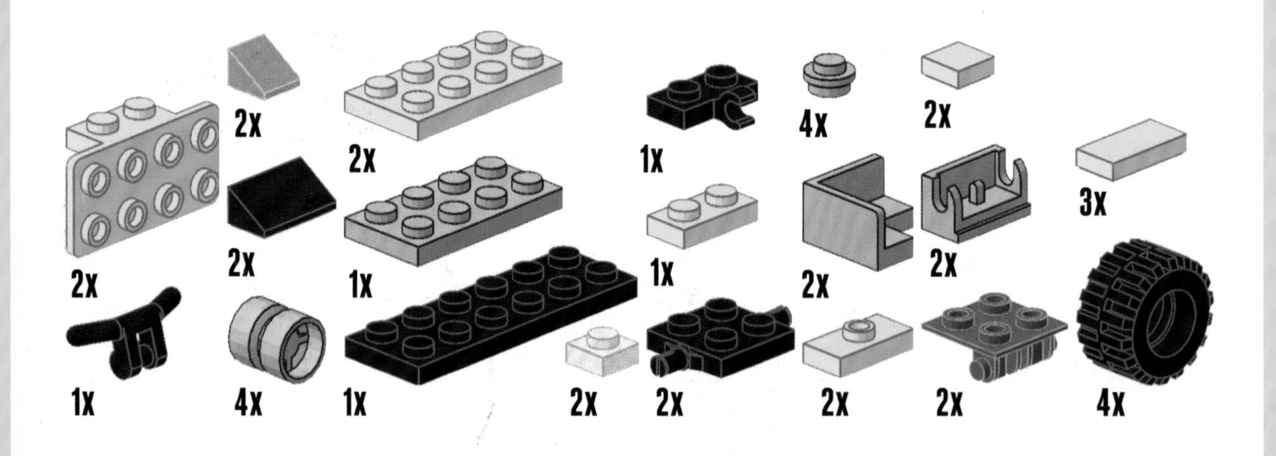

1

2

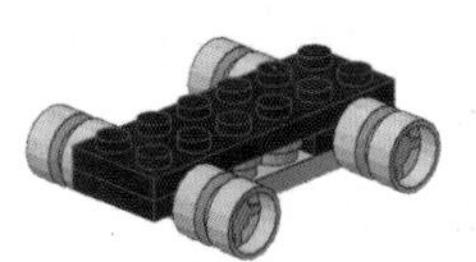

3

4

5

6

7

rolls-royce

For the biggest day of their lives, many couples choose to arrive at their wedding ceremony in something special. A popular choice is to hire a vintage car—often a Rolls-Royce, which has distinctive curved wheel arches and radiators. Using curved slopes with a variety of angles, we have recreated those iconic sweeping wheel arches. Our model is in classic wedding white with plush red seats. We have set back the main body work of the car to create the running boards, so often seen on a Rolls-Royce. We finish it off by building the unmistakable radiator and flat front.

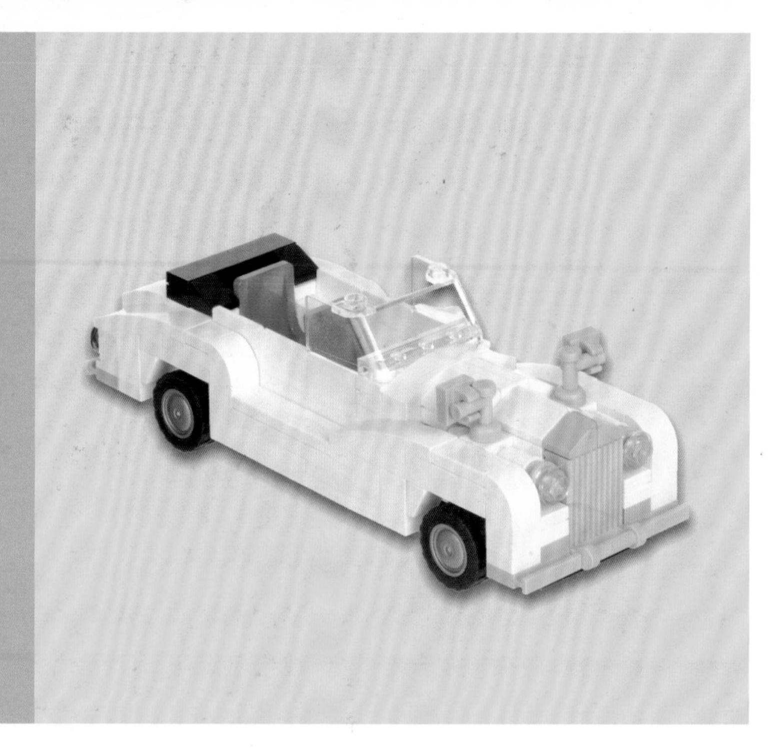

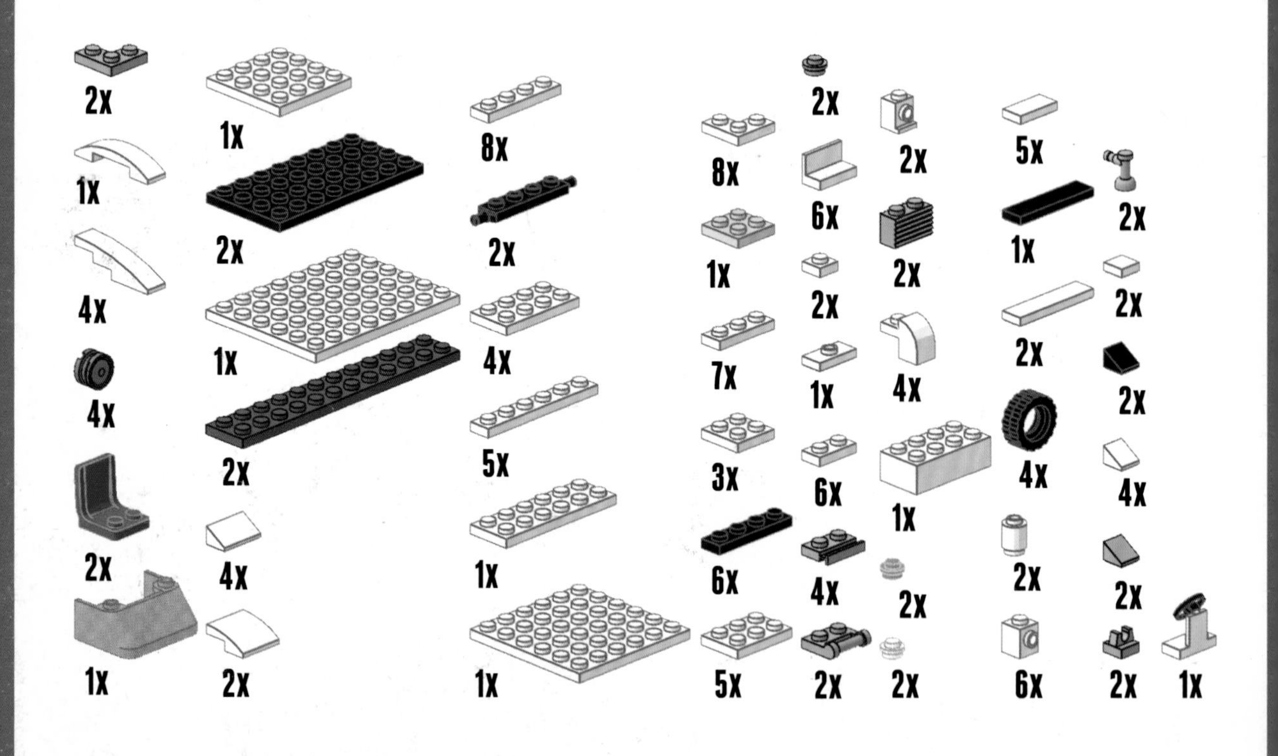

1

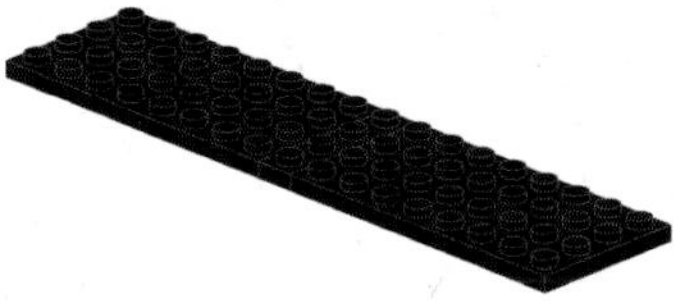

2

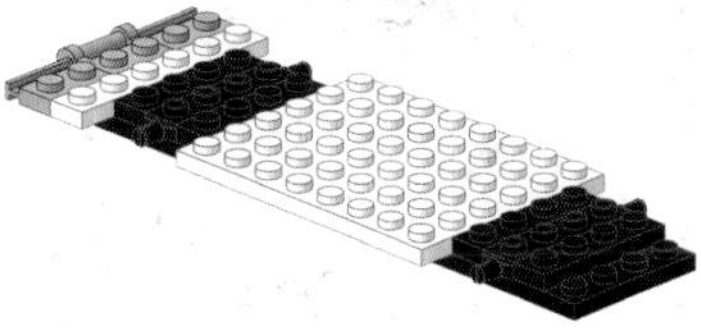

3

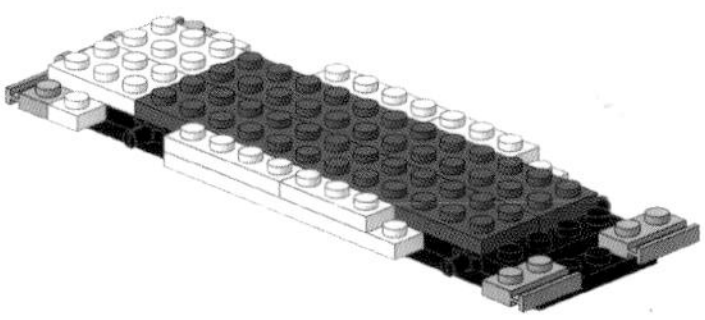

4

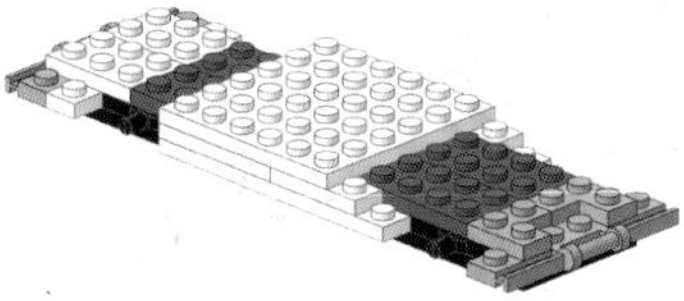

5

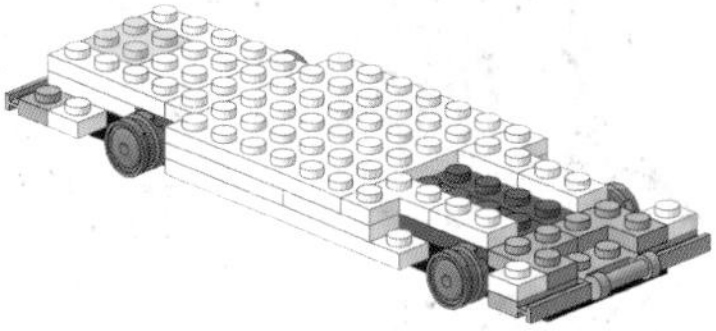

6

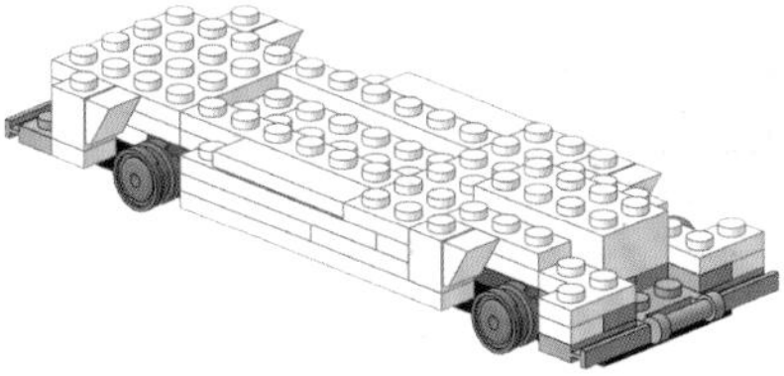

7

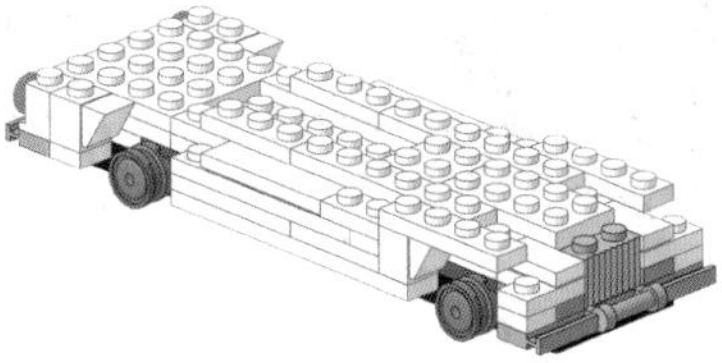

8

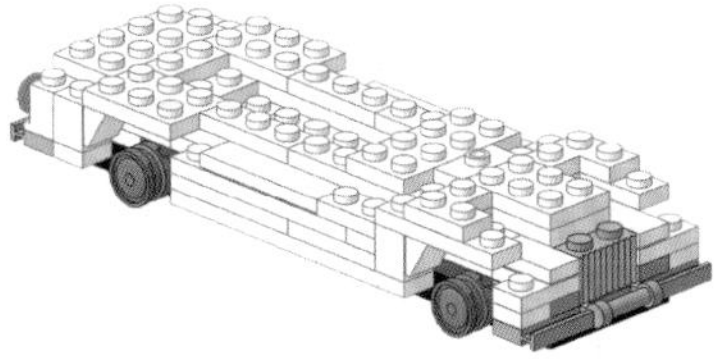

9

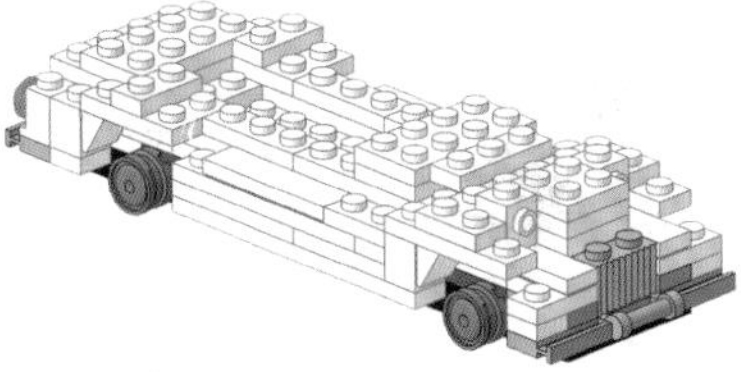

10

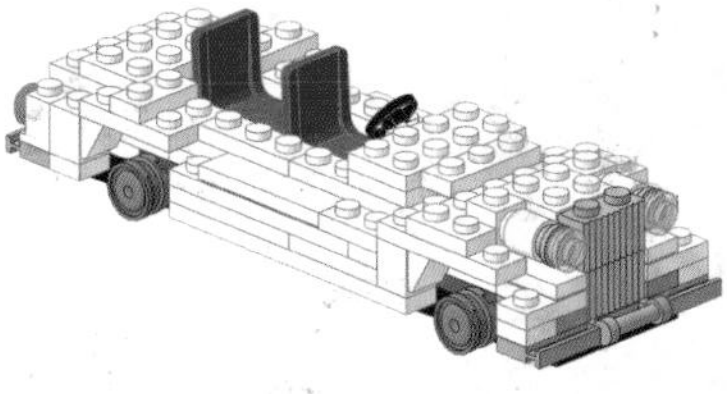

11

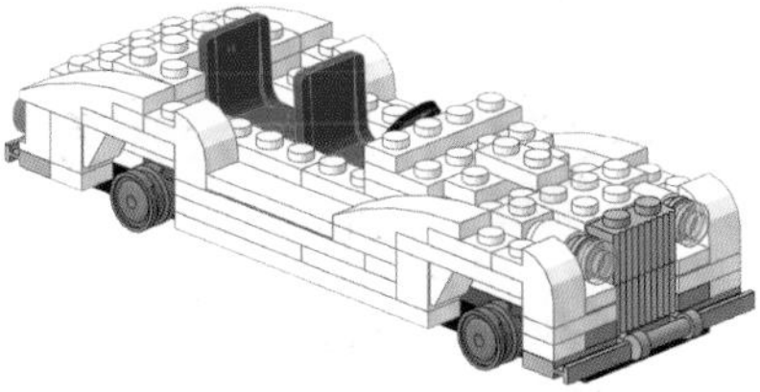

12

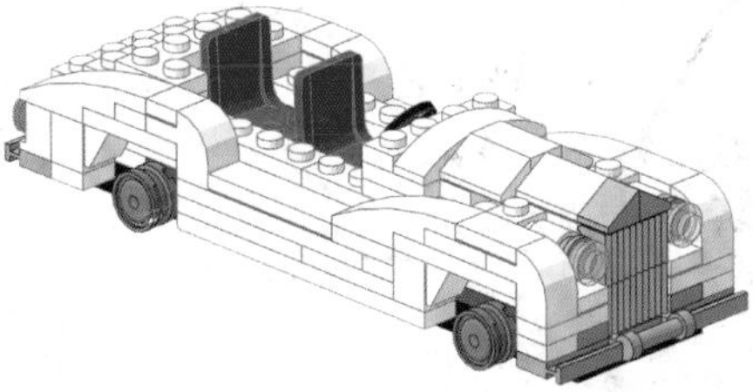

13

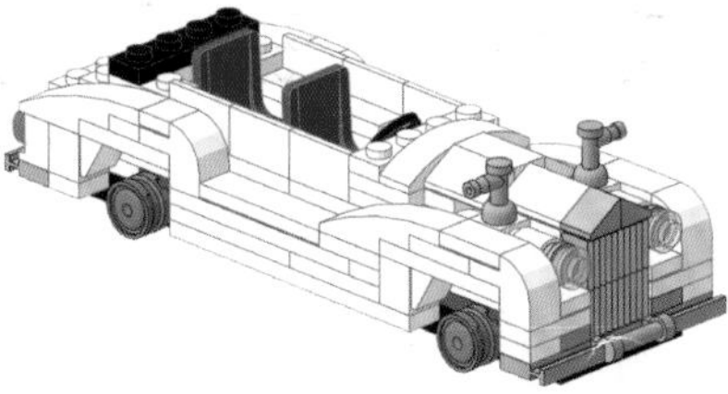

14

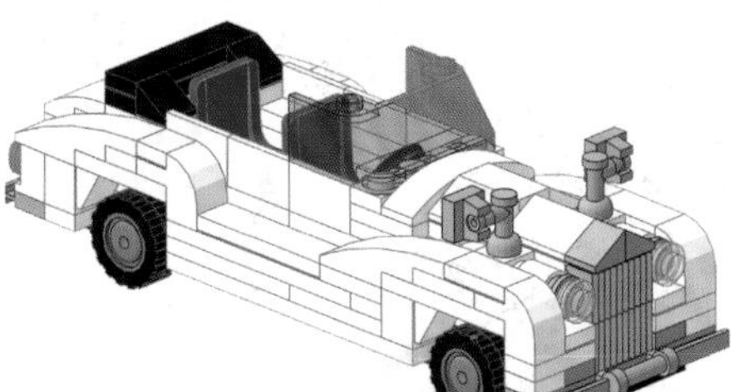

tanker truck

Designed to carry anything from gasoline and milk to bulk dry goods such as flour and gases, tanker trucks are tightly sealed containers mounted onto trailer units. The hatches on the roof are used for loading and unloading the cargo via hoses. For our tanker truck, we've used a combination of 1 x 2 and 1 x 4 curved slopes to recreate its wonderful curved roof. For the perfect base we used 2 x 2 double jumper plates and 1 x 1 round tiles make up the hatch covers.

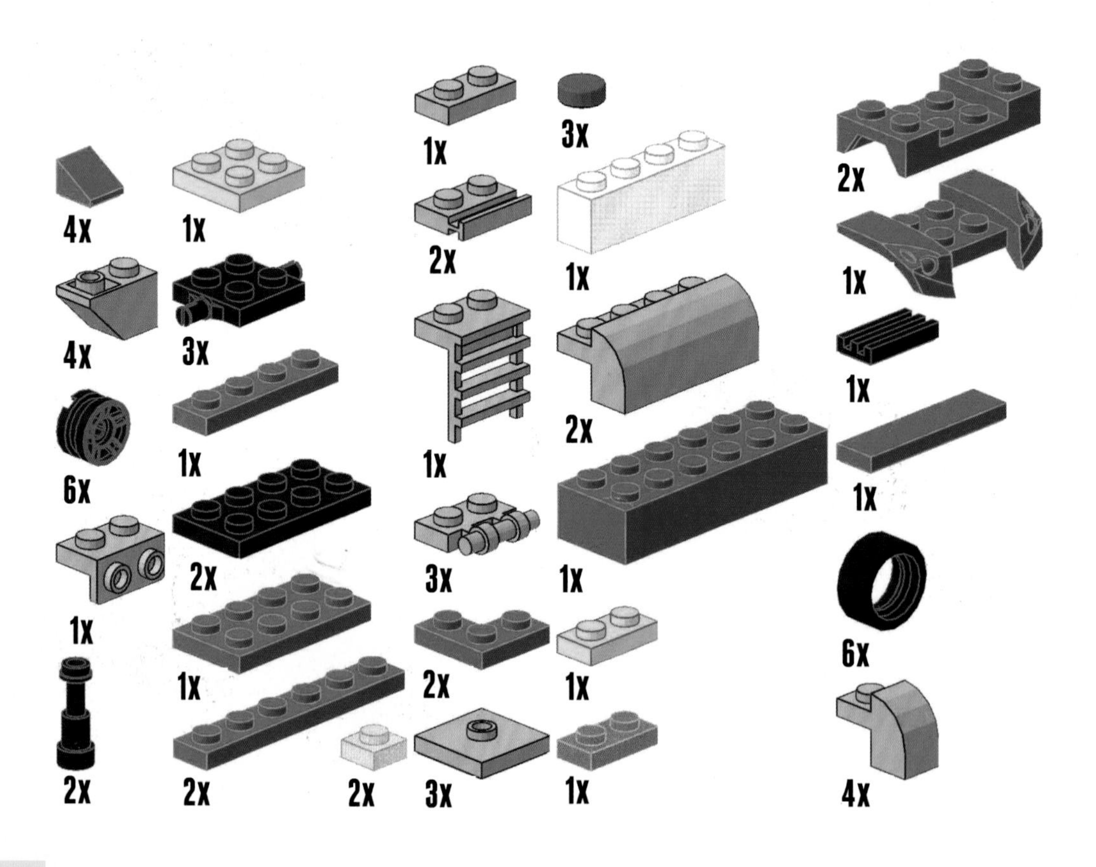

1

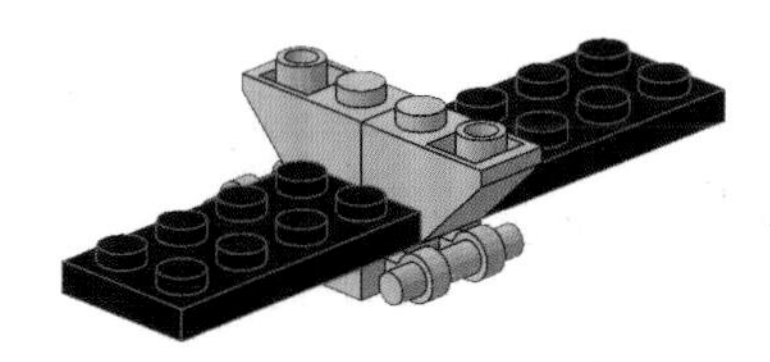

2

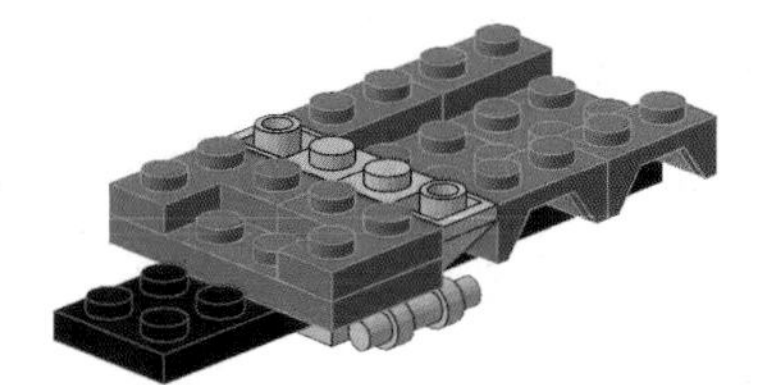

3

4

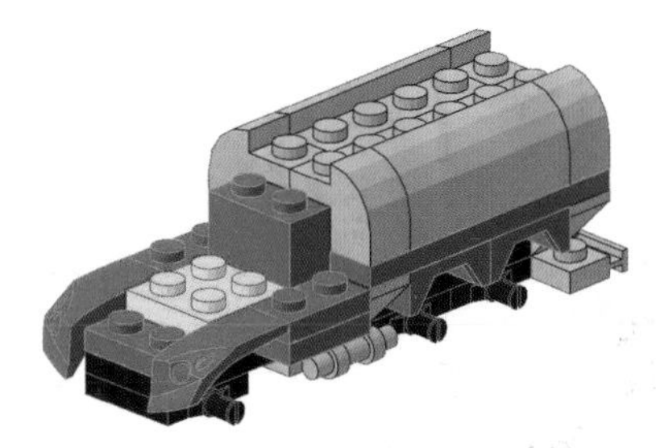

5

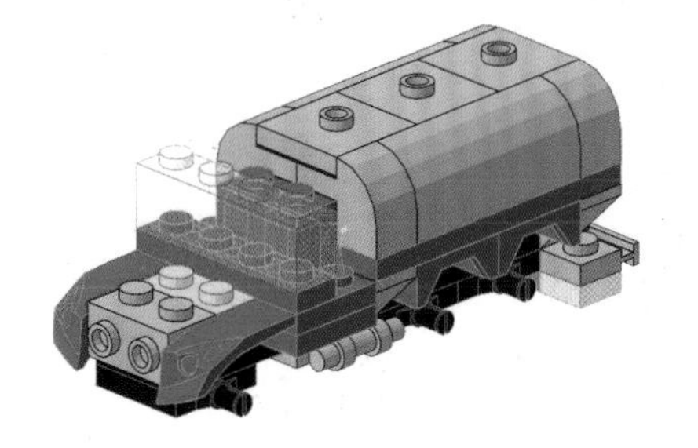

6

tractor

The tractor is the farmer's friend, used to work the land across the world. Its powerful engines and massive rear wheels give it the grip it needs to work in muddy fields—come rain or shine. Like most tractors, our cheery green model has an open top with a roll-cage, offering the driver extra protection in case he has an accident. Tractors can be adapted to carry a huge variety of farm equipment, on both the front and back. As the tractor's driving position is so high up, we've used 1 x 2 plates to create steps up to the driving seat.

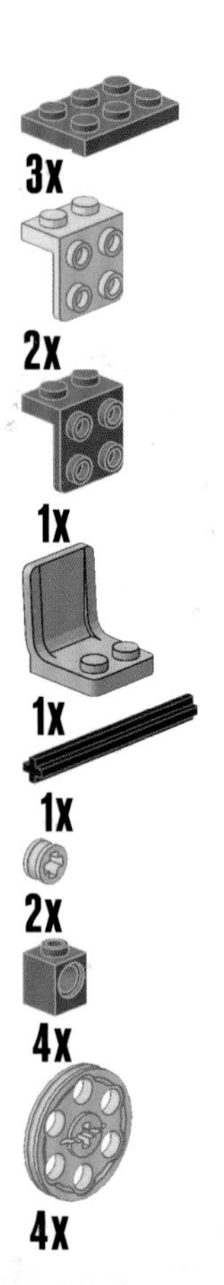

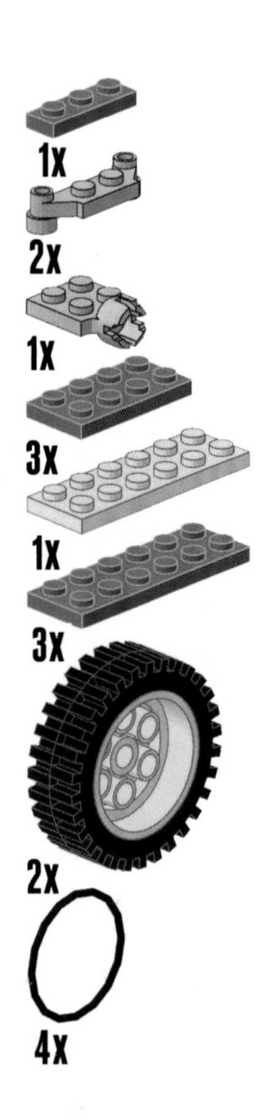

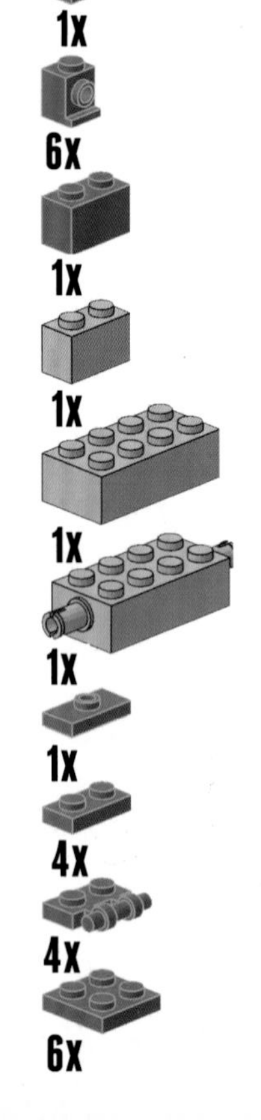

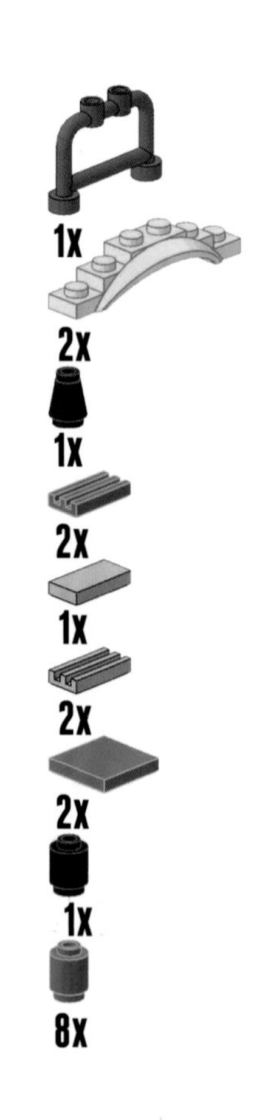

1

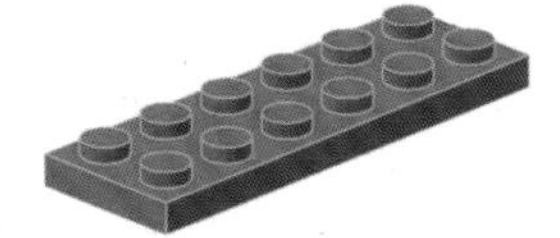

2

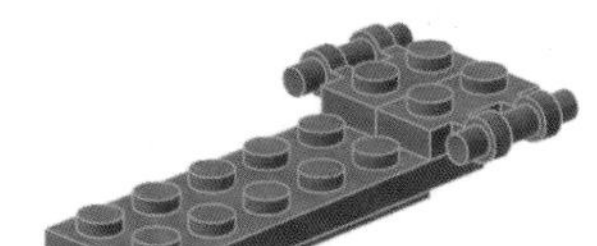

3

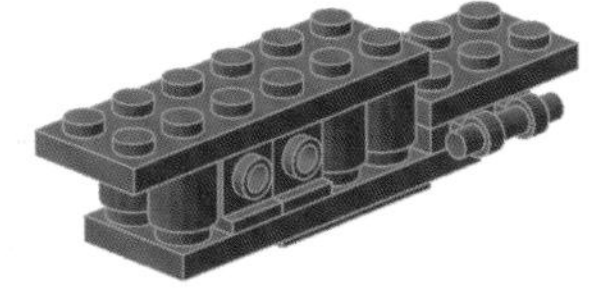

4

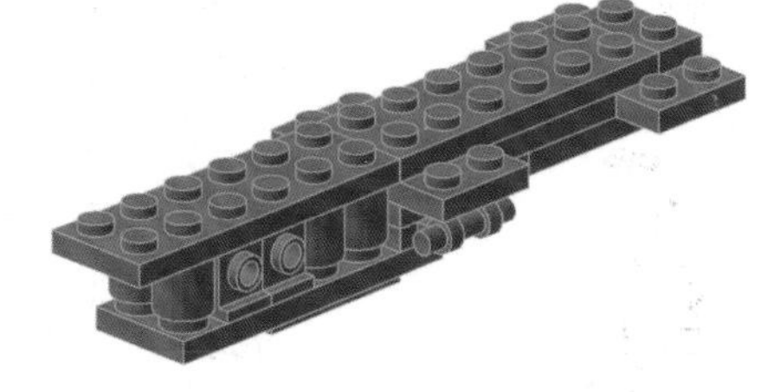

5

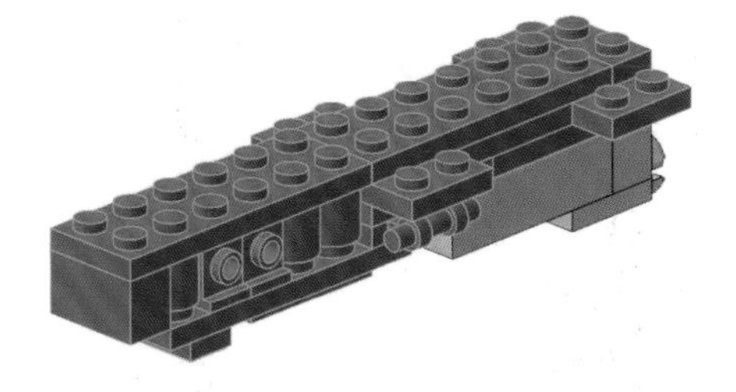

6

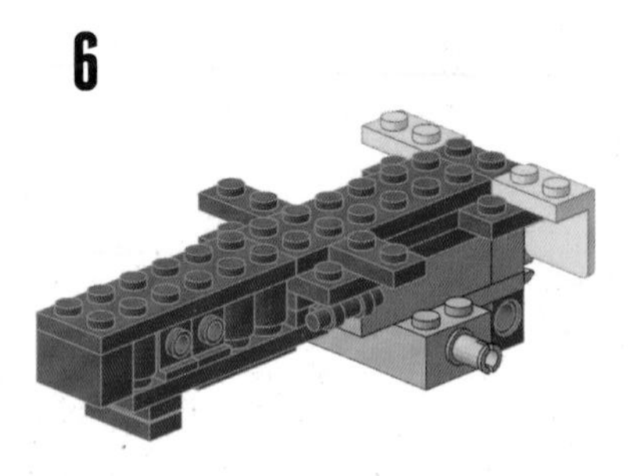

7

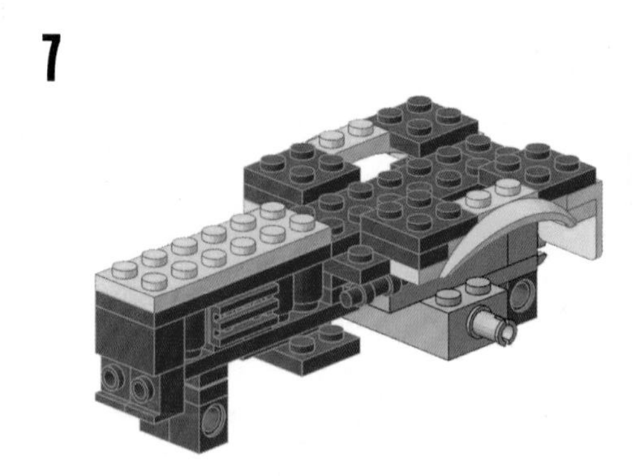

8

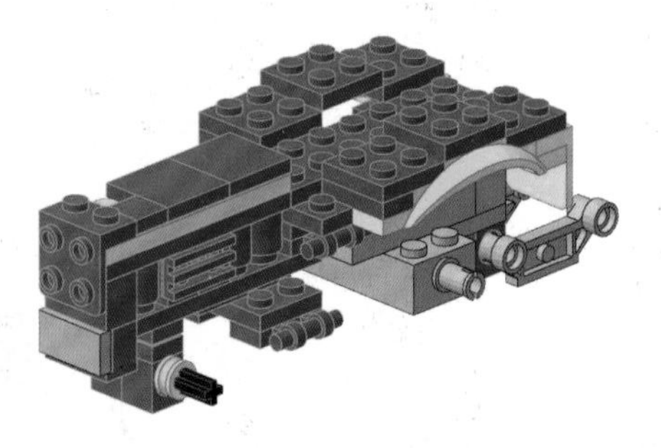

9

bulldozer

Need to flatten a building or clear some land? Then call in the bulldozer! This tractor—with two large tracks on either side and a big blade at the front—is designed to push large piles of soil or rubble out of the way. These powerful vehicles also often have a rear-mounted claw to break up very hard material. We have used curved slopes to give our yellow bulldozer the snub-nose that makes them so recognizable. The 1 x 2 grill tiles recreate the vents on either side of the engine and the front radiator.

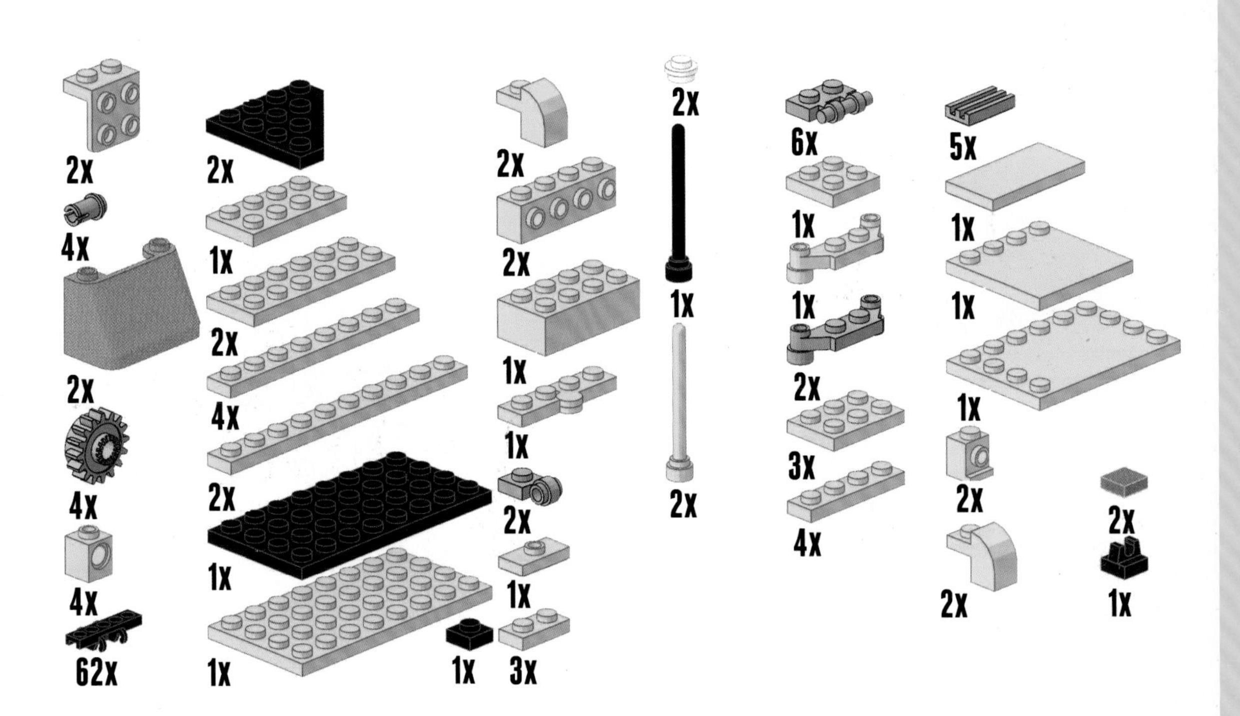

1

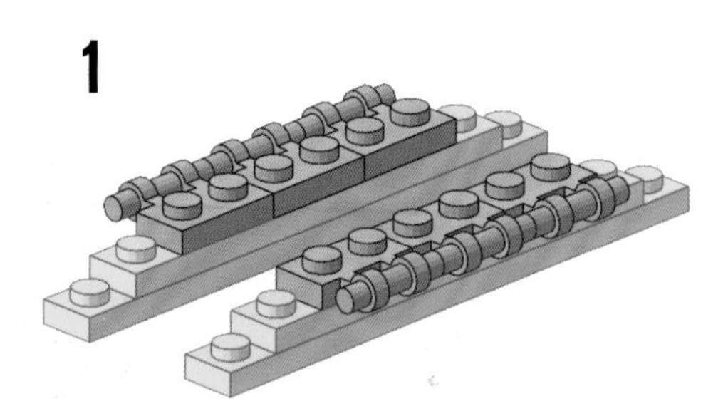

2

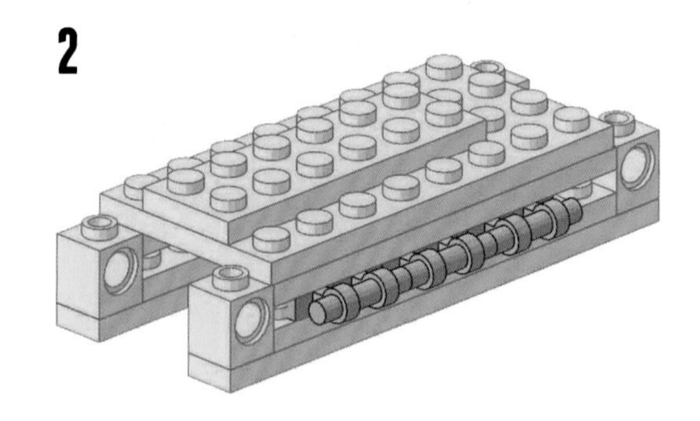

3

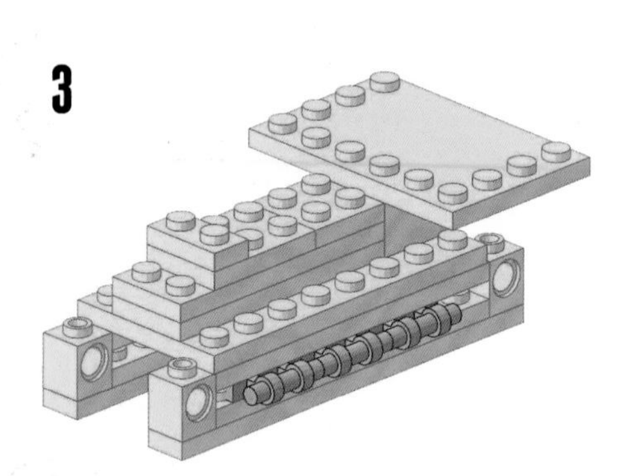

4

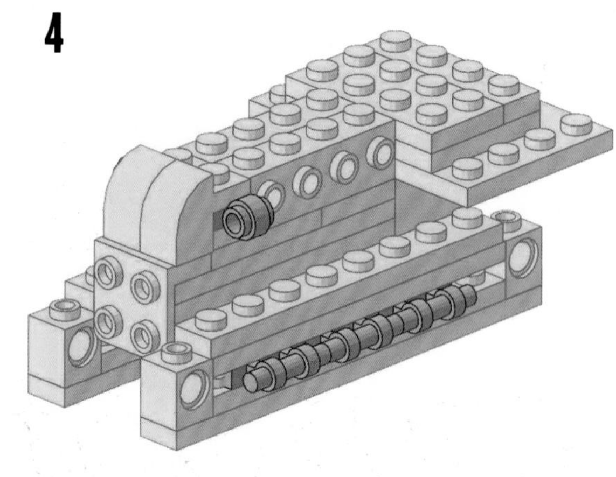

5

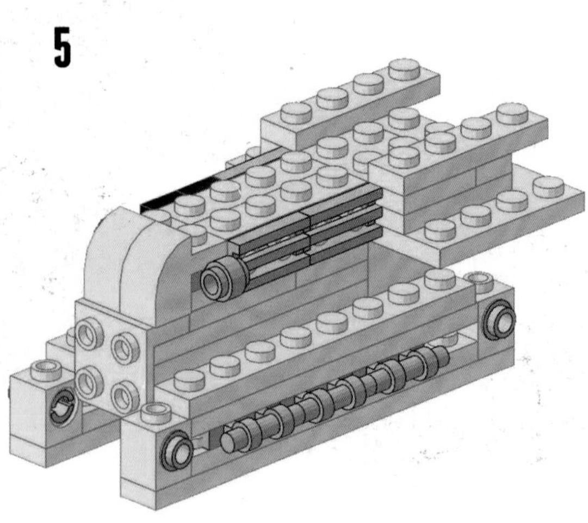

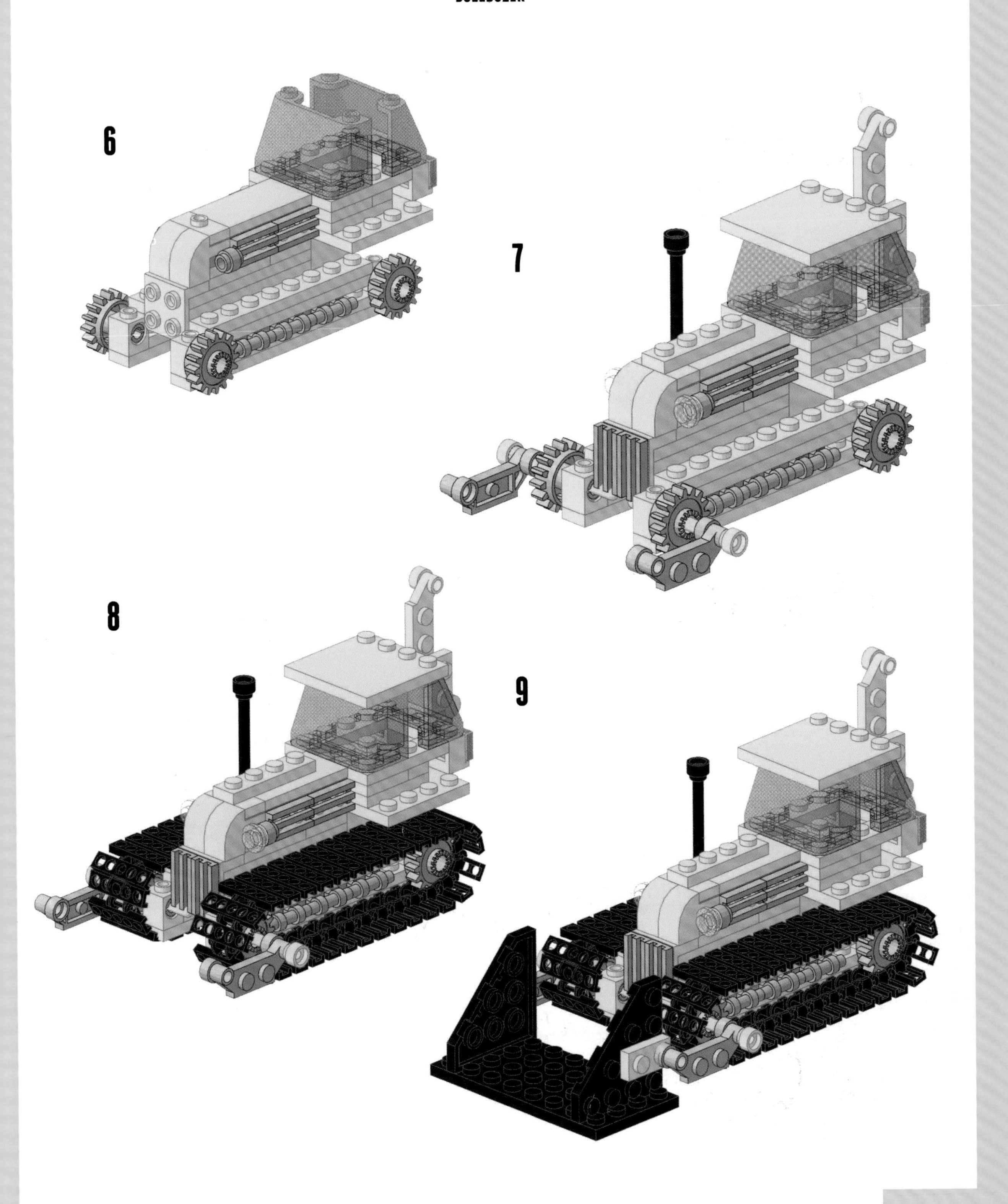
6
7
8
9

dump truck

These big vehicles are used to transport bulk loads of gravel or sand in one go and dump them where needed. They're most commonly seen on construction sites and in mines—anyplace where heavy loads need moving from A to B. The "dump" part of the truck is made up of a tip-up, open-ended container behind the driver's cab. For our model we've put the dump section above two axles' worth of solid wheels, which are designed to cope with a heavy load.

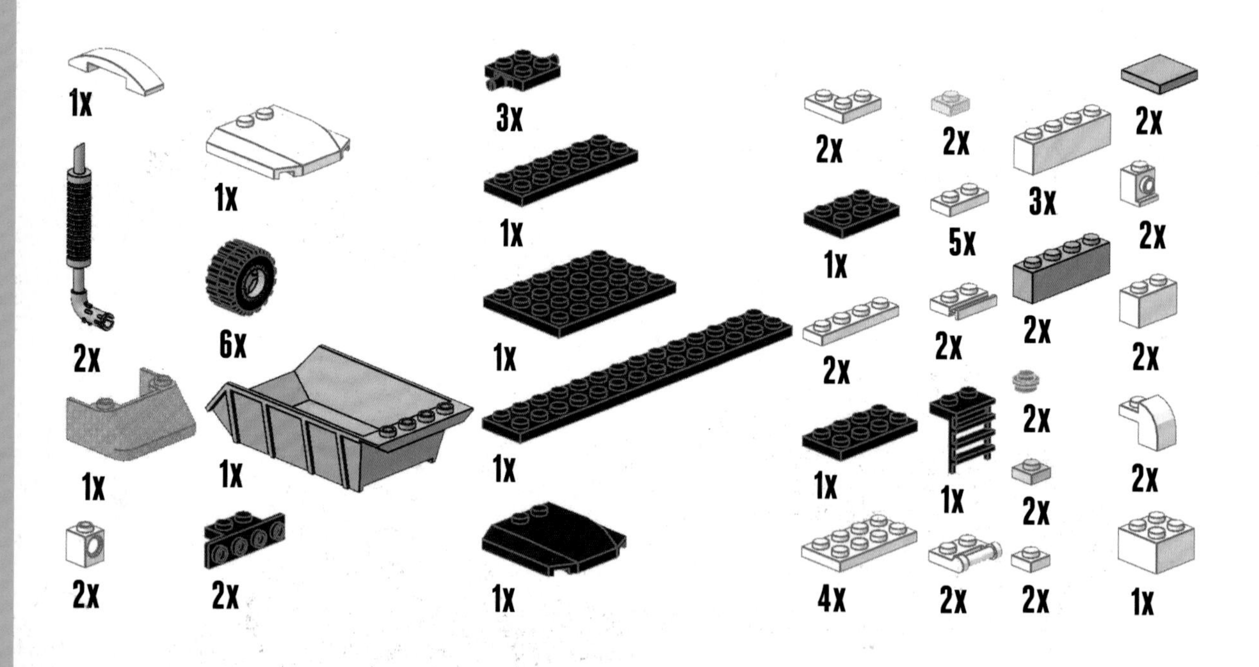

1

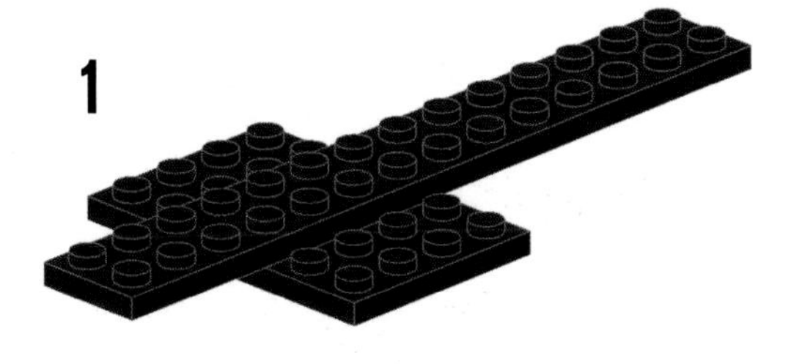

2

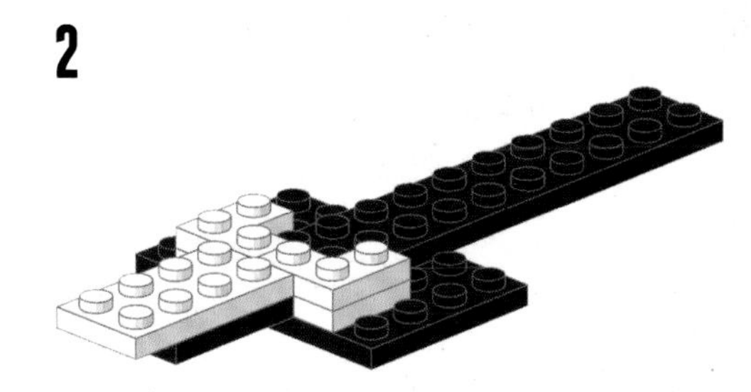

3

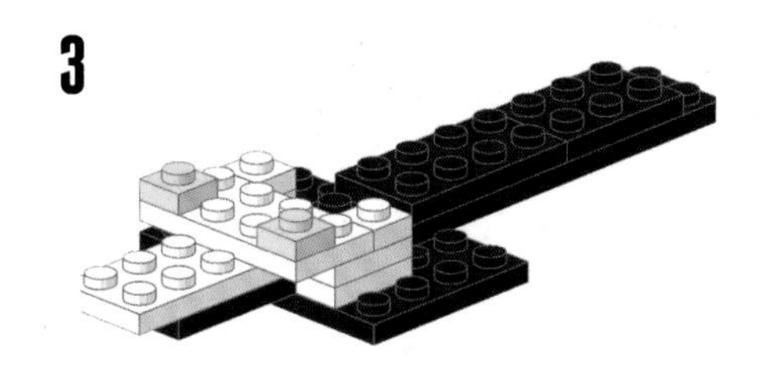

4

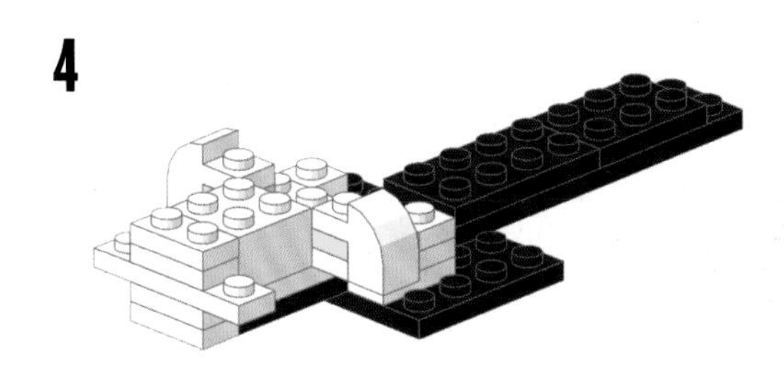

5

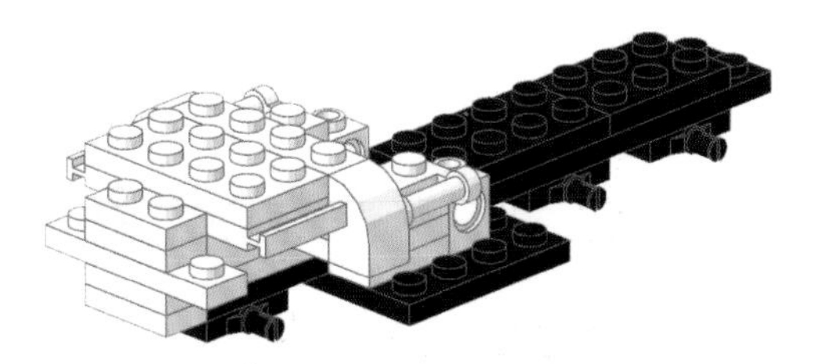

6

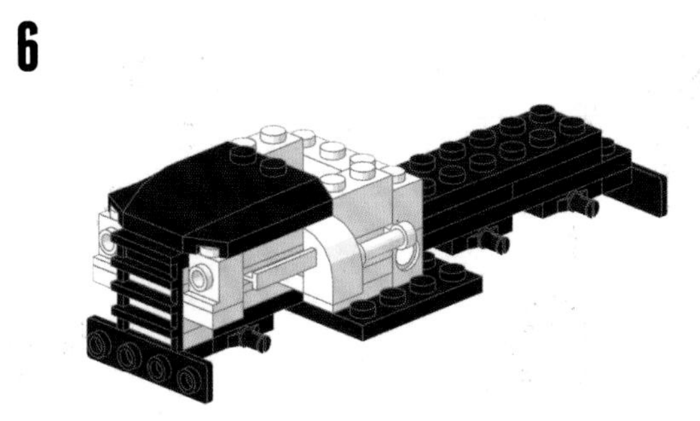

7

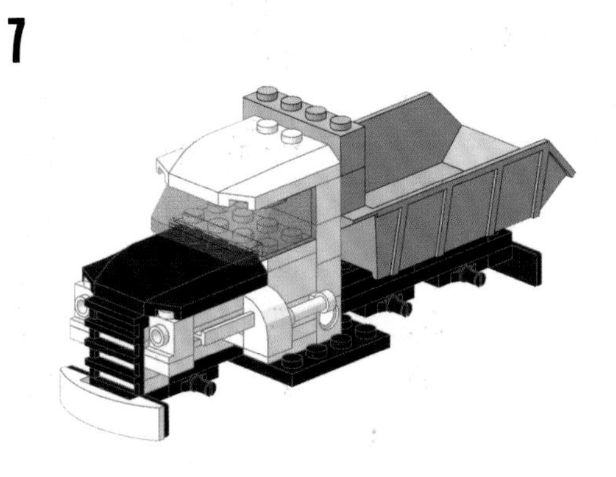

8

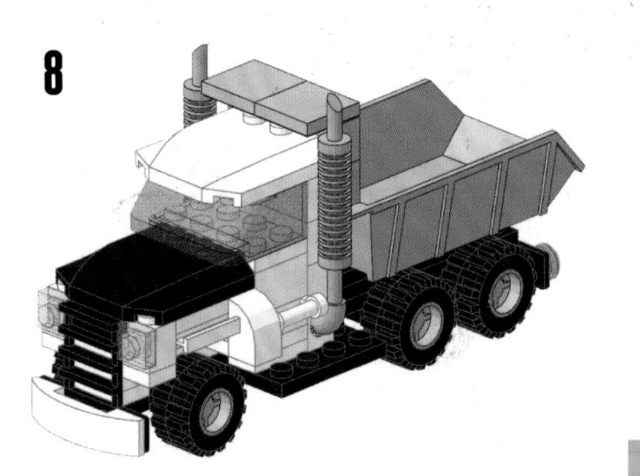

ford model t

It's often said that Henry Ford deemed his cars could be "any color as long as it's black," but in actuality the original Model T was available in many different colors, and the cars have been painted into almost every color since. Our LEGO® model is based on a 1927 model, which still exists—on display at the Henry Ford Museum in Detroit, Michigan.

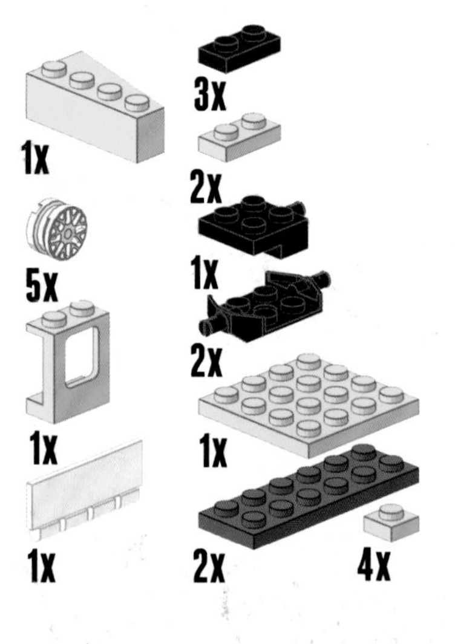

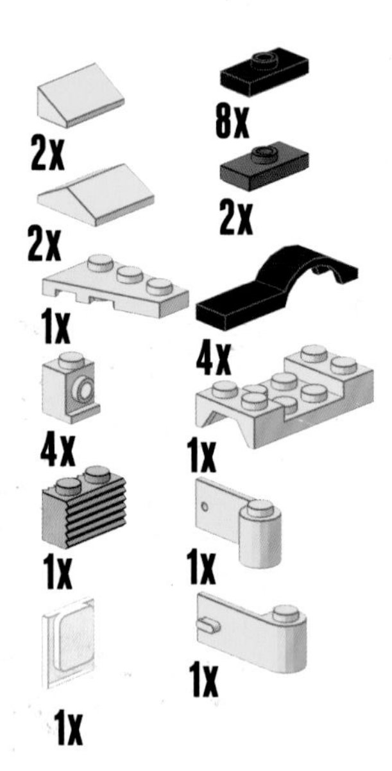

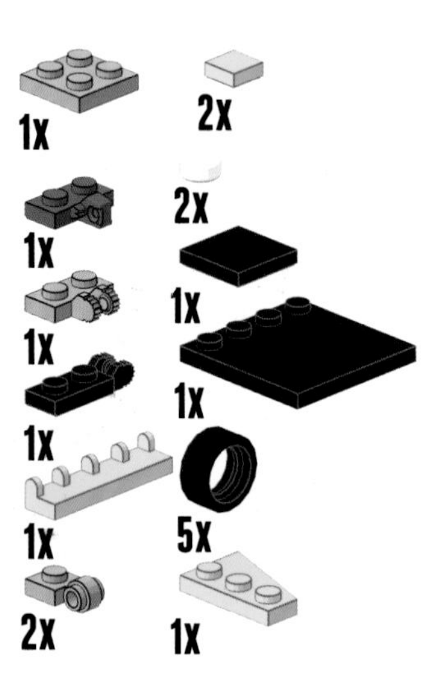

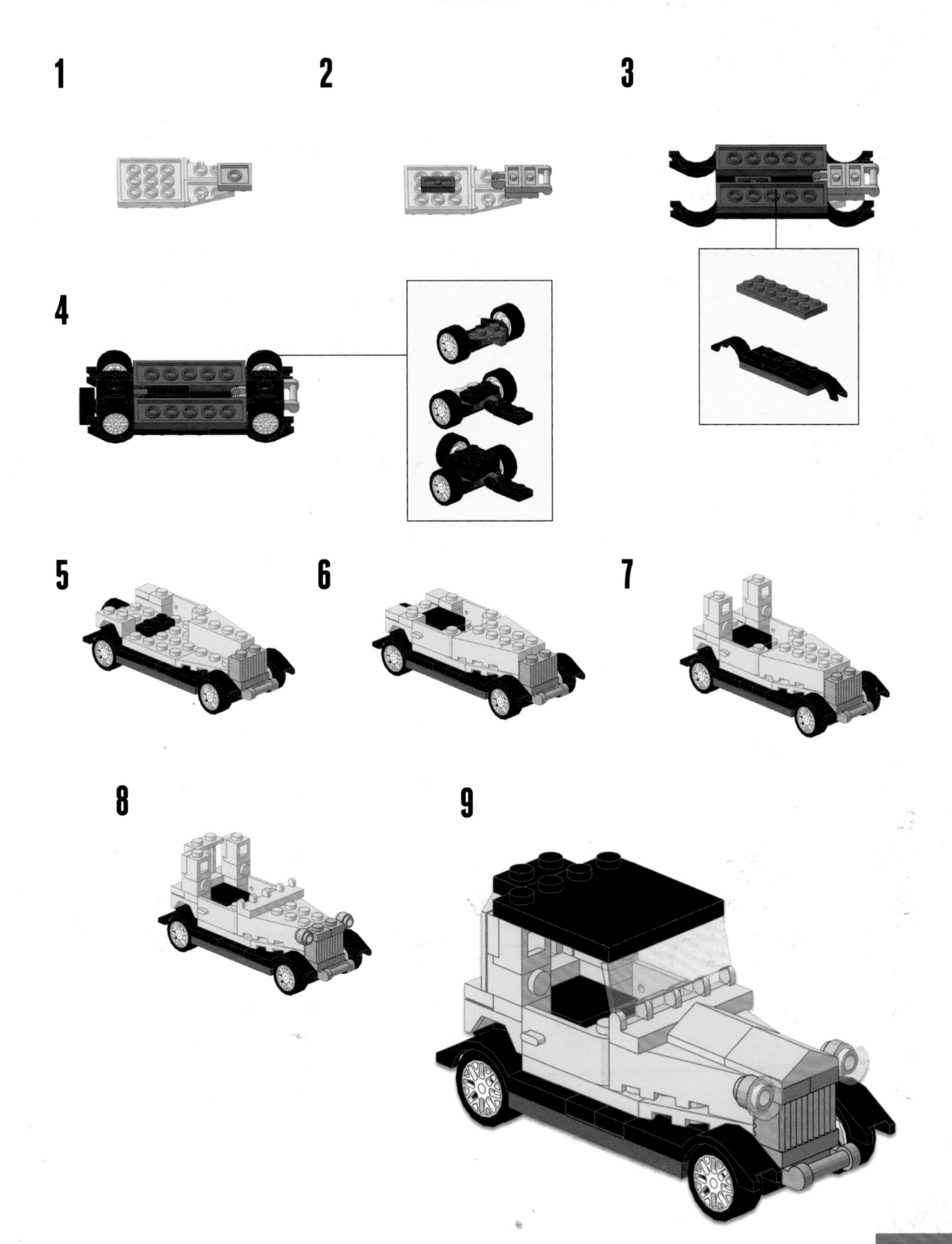
1
2
3
4
5
6
7
8
9

cherry picker

Originally named after the equipment used to pick fruit from the top of a cherry tree, these mobile, aerial platforms are used for all kinds of jobs, from fixing street lamps to putting up decorations. They are made up of a bucket fitted to the end of a moving arm, which can be lifted into the air. They come in all shapes and sizes, but most are small and easy to move, much like the one we've created. To recreate the 360-degree movement of the boom arm, we've used a 2 x 2 turntable, positioned in the center, to give us a solid base. For the bucket, we have used a specially designed piece from another model kit.

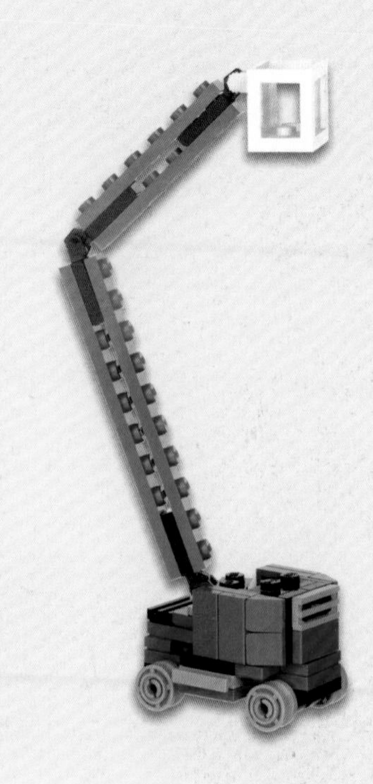

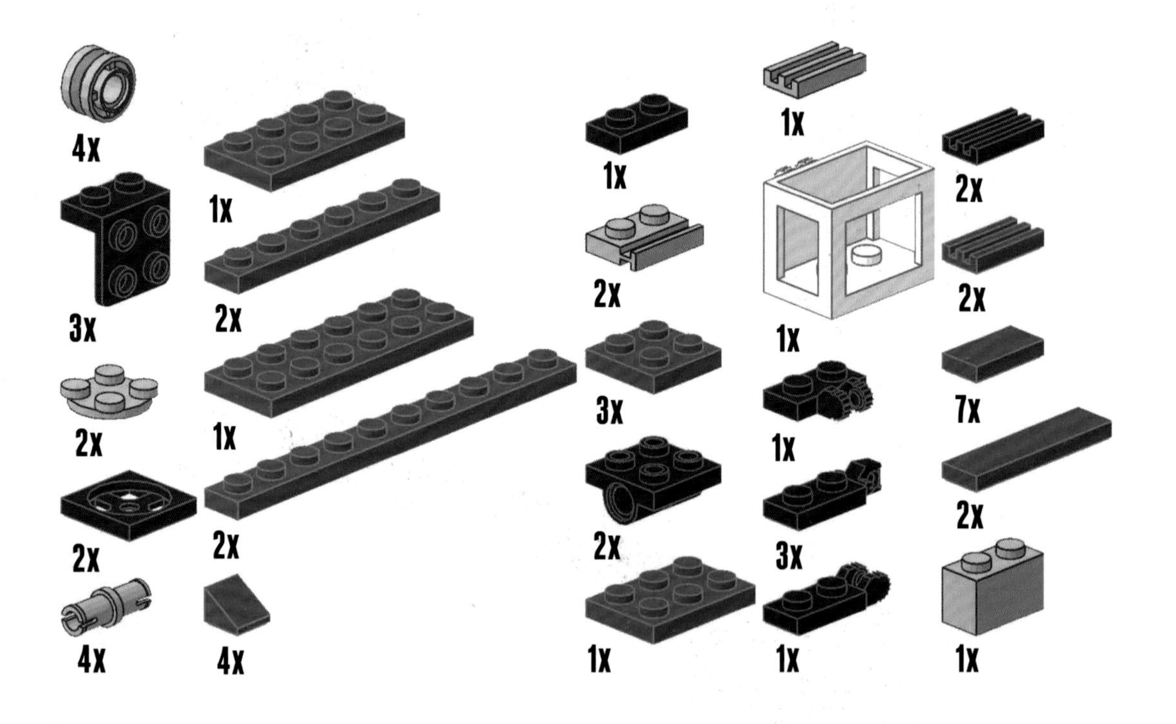

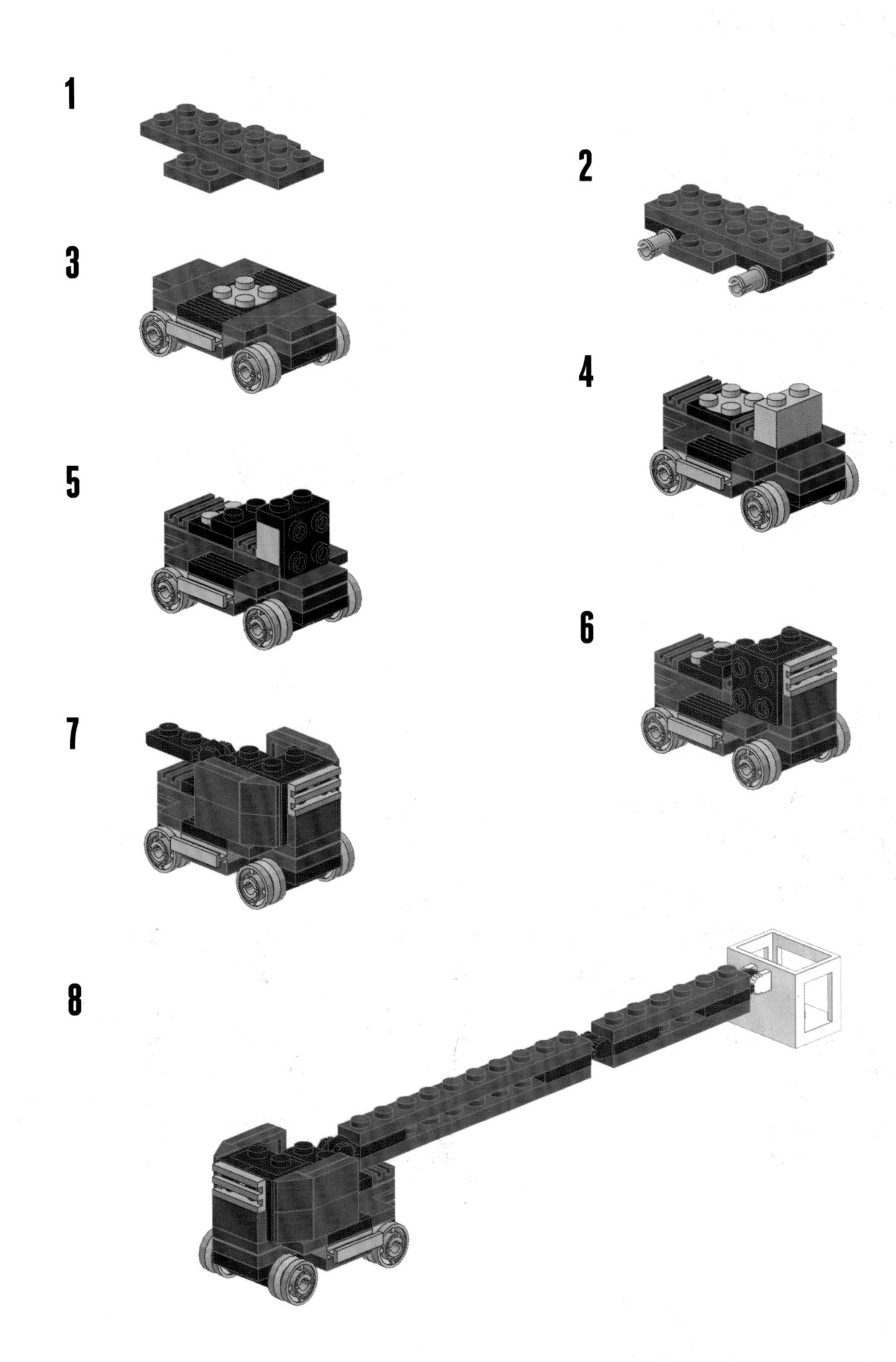
1
2
3
4
5
6
7
8

smart car

Smart cars are a range of micro- and sub-compact cars perfect for city driving. They're instantly recognizable by their super-compact design. In fact, they're so small you can park lengthwise in a space the same size as the width of a regular car! While they might look like a real-life LEGO® model, they actually have space for two passengers and sometimes come with four seats. The original smart car was white, but we've chosen to make our model in a lovely blue. We've used the cheese slope piece to perfectly capture the snub-nosed hood slopes.

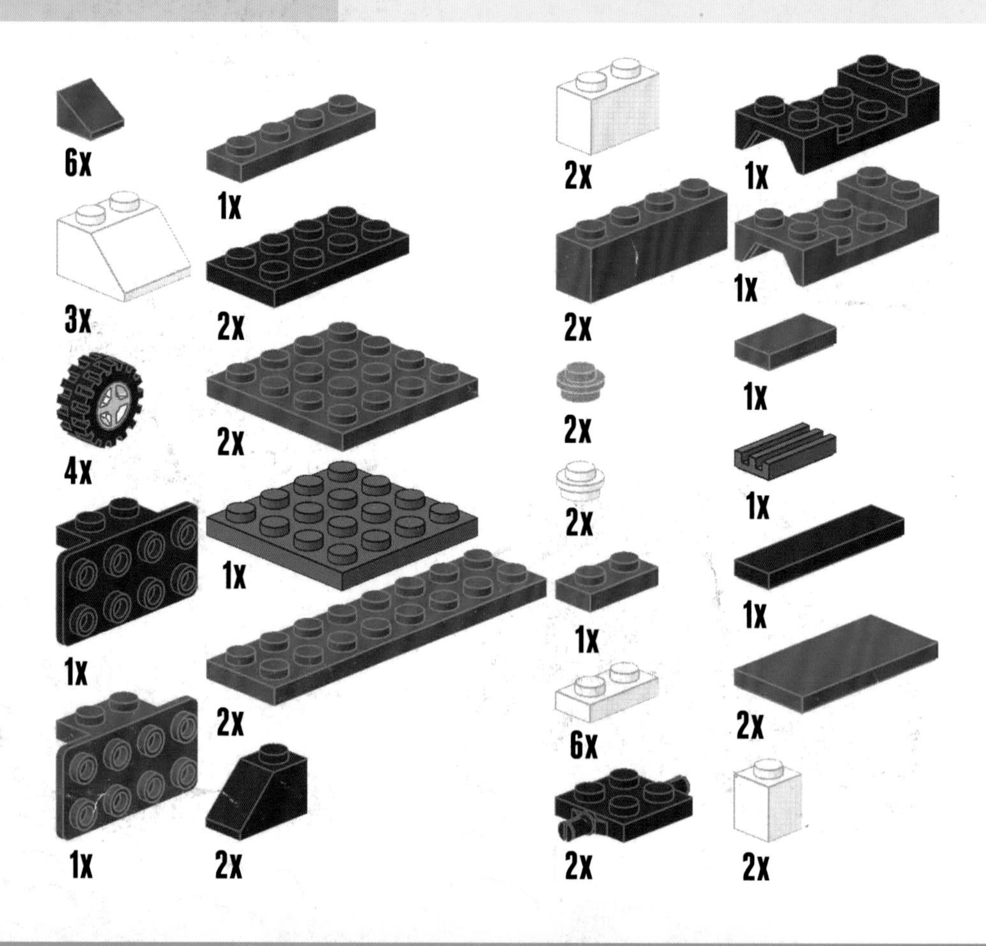

1

2

3

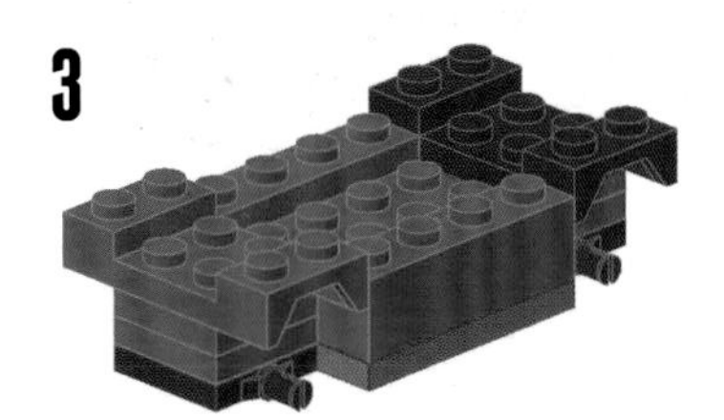

4

5

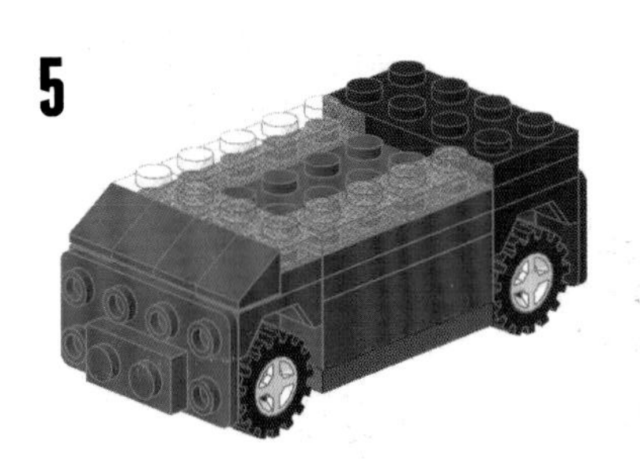

6

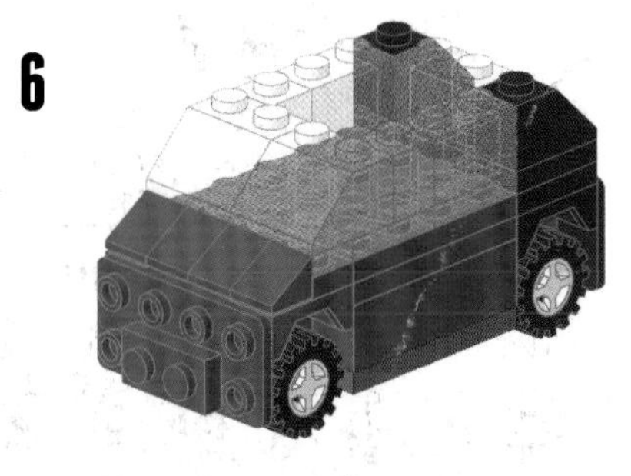

7

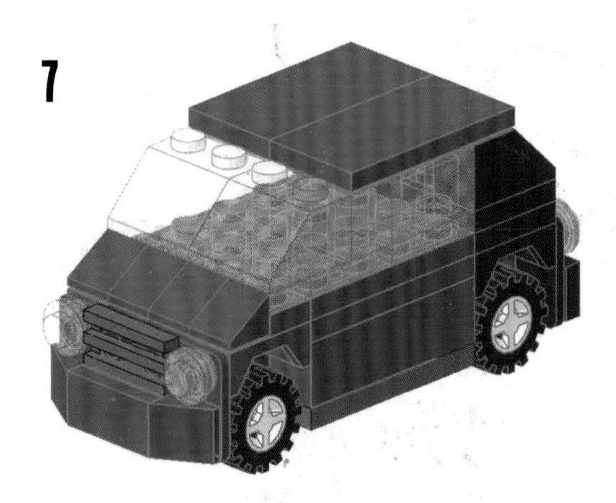

mini cooper

The MINI is a real icon of 1960s Britain. Made famous by the Michael Caine movie, *The Italian Job*, where three MINIs take part in a daring car chase—complete with epic stunts—its agile handling and eye-catching style make it one of Britain's most popular cars. It was manufactured by the British Motor Company from 1959 until 2000, when BMW bought and remodeled it. In a 1999 poll, the MINI was voted the second most influential car of the 20th century, only beaten by the Ford Model T.

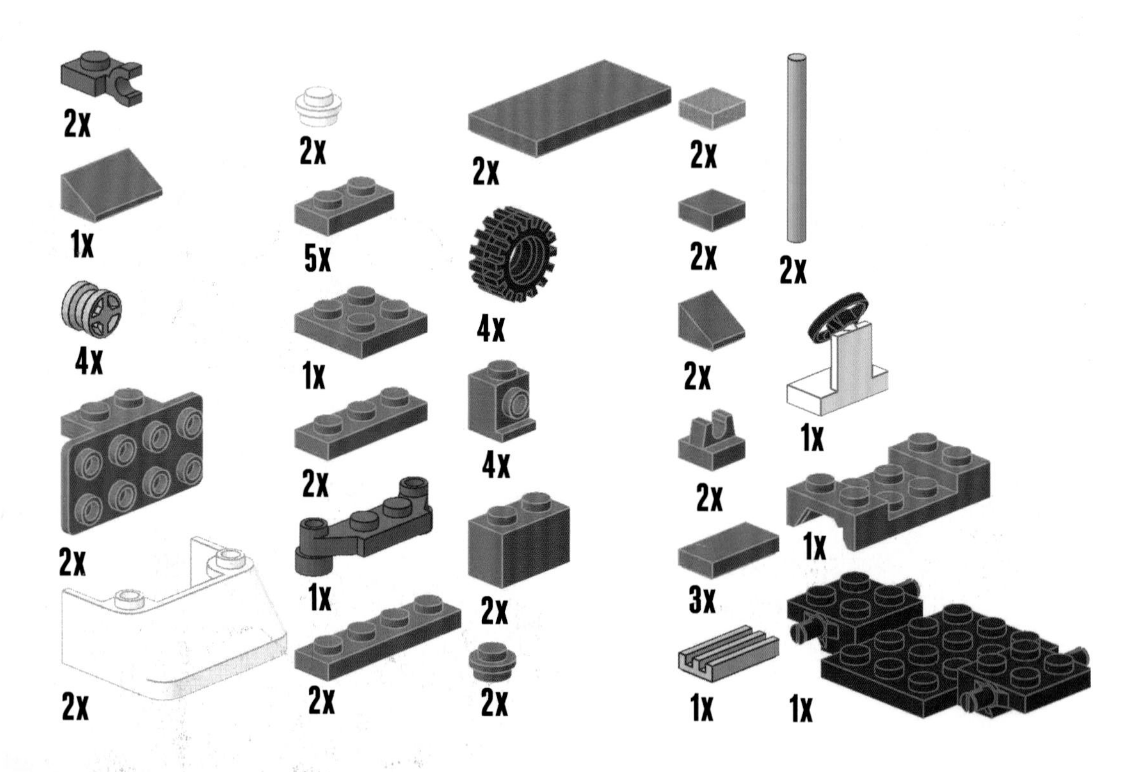

1

2

3

4

5

6

7

8

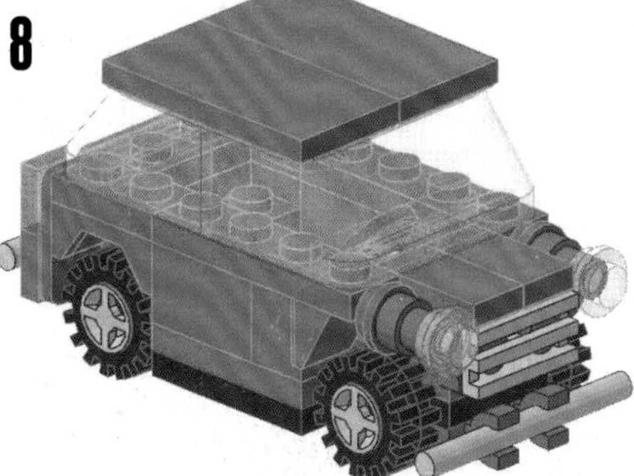

taxi

Whether you're off to the airport, on a night out, or just going to work, you can usually find a taxi to take you there. Used to transport people the world over, taxis come in all shapes and sizes. New York's famous yellow taxis grace the sets of countless movies, and London's black cab is an image of quintessential Britain. We've decided to make the former at a micro-scale and used small cheese slope pieces for the iconic advertising sign on top.

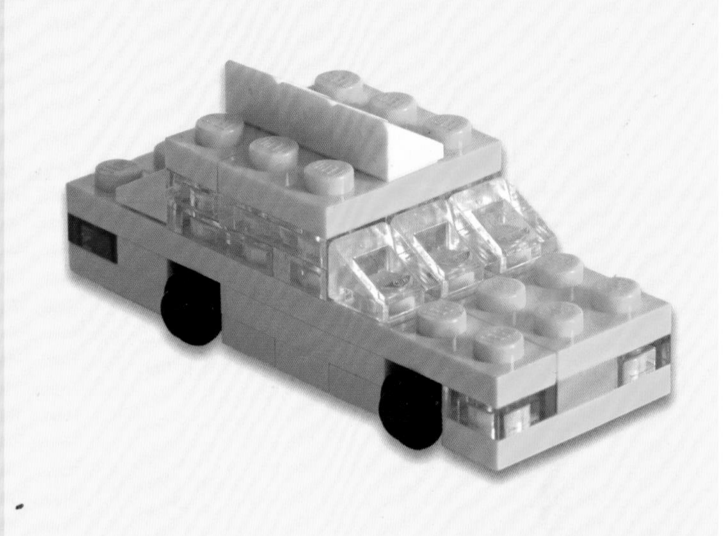

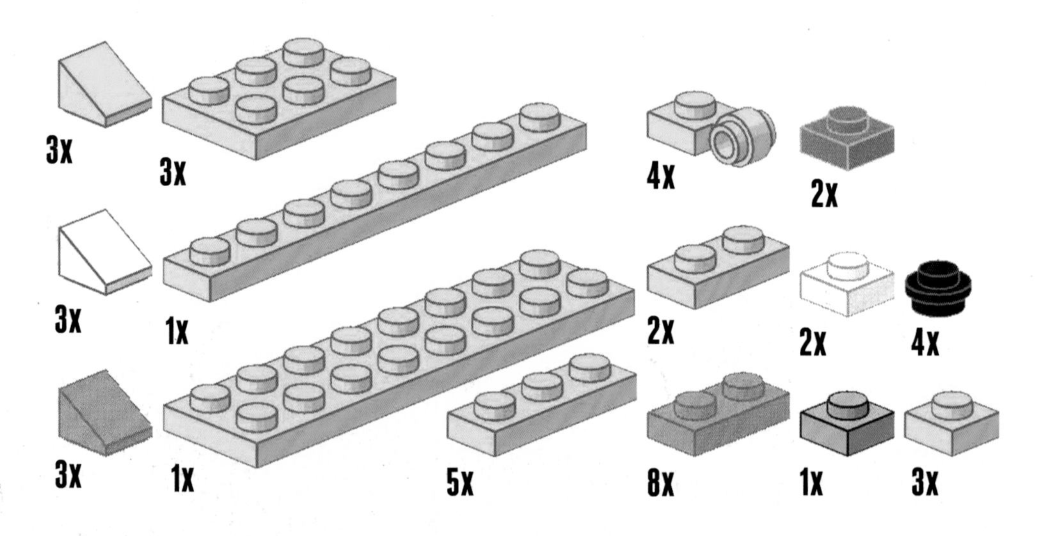

1

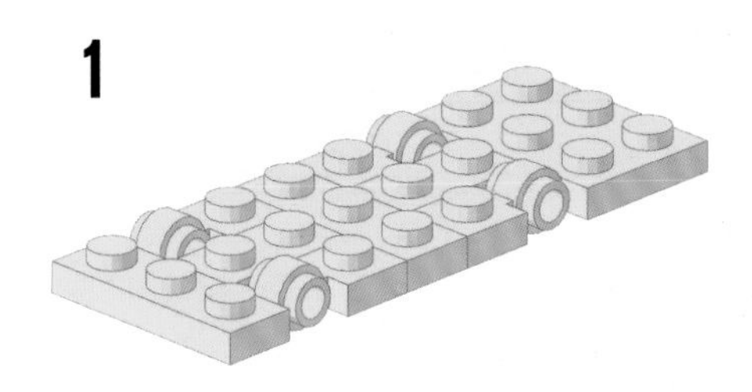

2

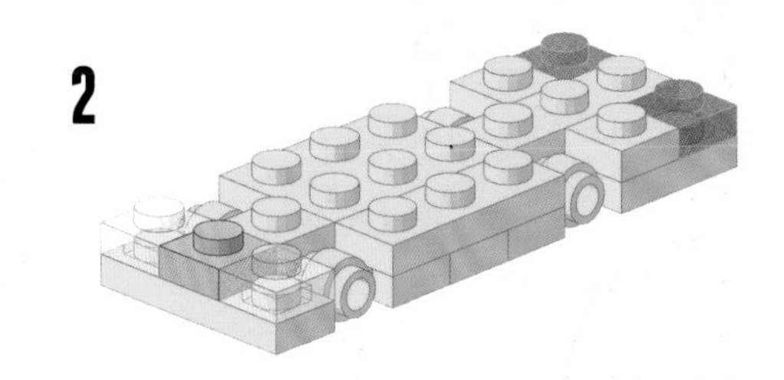

3

4

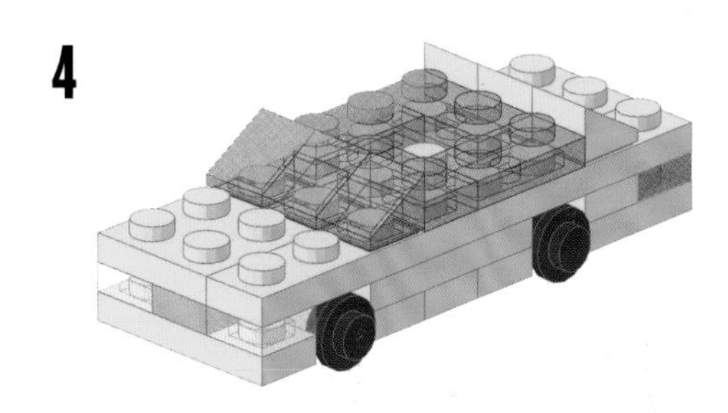

5

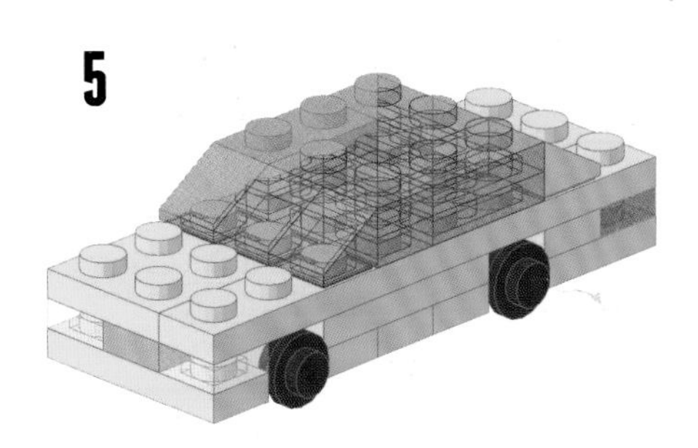

6

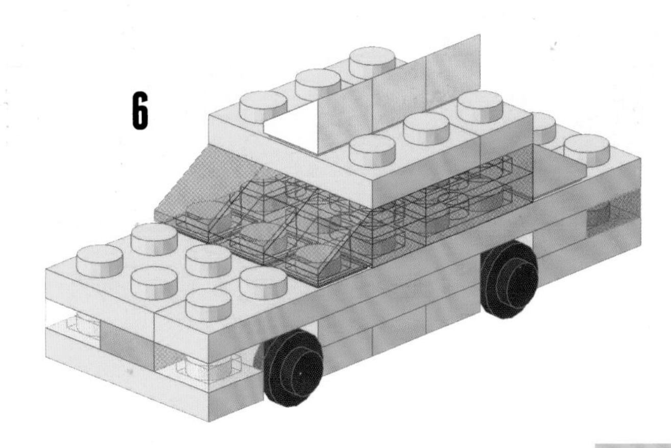

tuk tuk

A native of India, Indonesia, Nigeria, Mozambique, and Tanzania, this little three-wheeled taxi is a common sight carrying passengers around town. They are agile enough to weave between vehicles and beat heavy traffic to take people where they want to go, fast. They might be compact, but there's enough space for a driver and a passenger, so we've used two 4 x 4 curved plates to create the canopy covering both of them. The basic seat, which is usually no more than a bench, is built using four 1 x 2 cheese slopes.

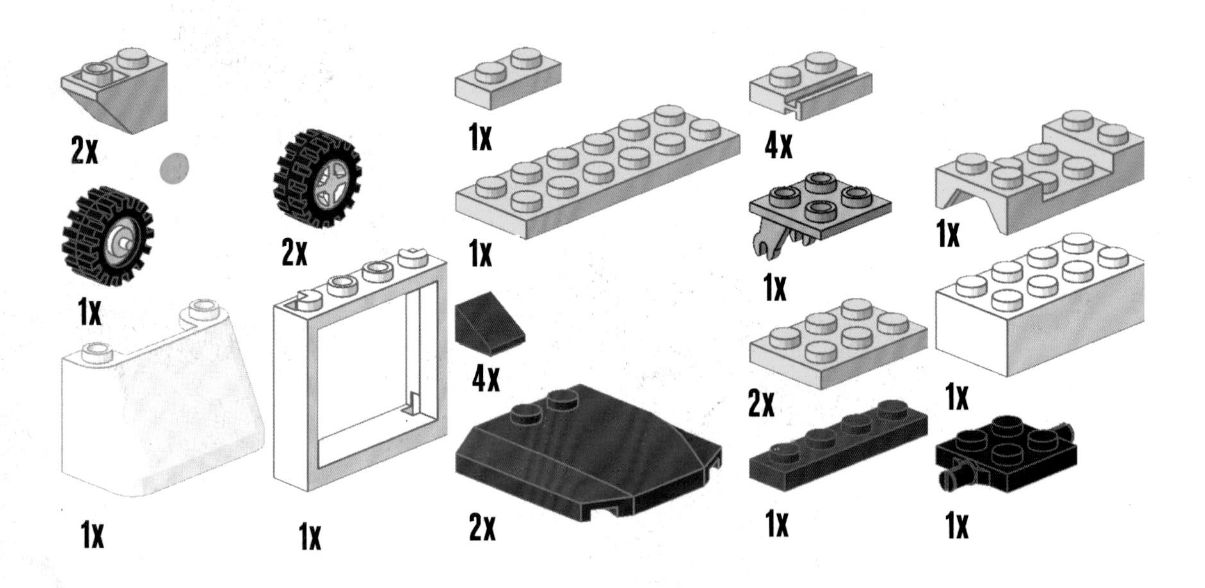

1

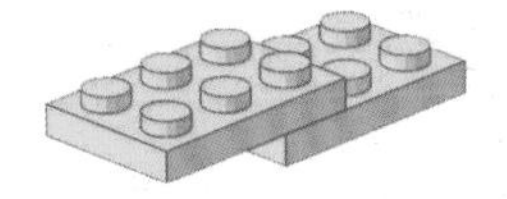

2

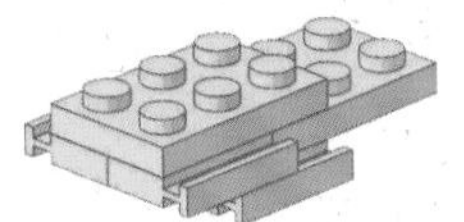

3

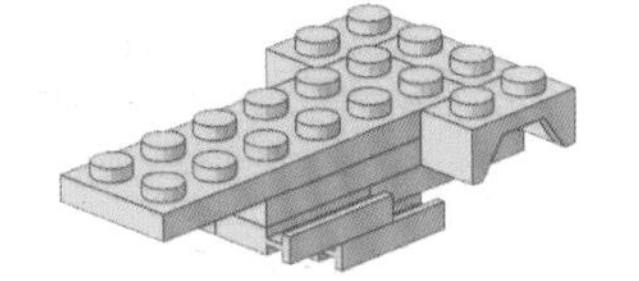

4

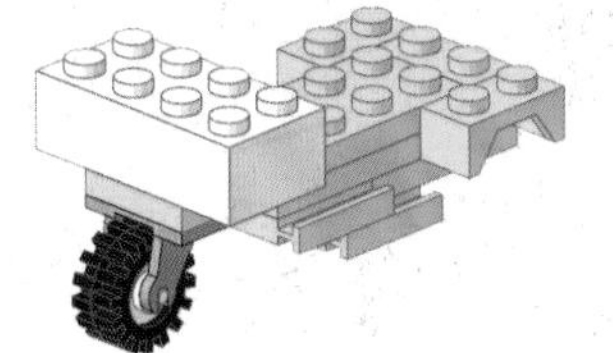

5

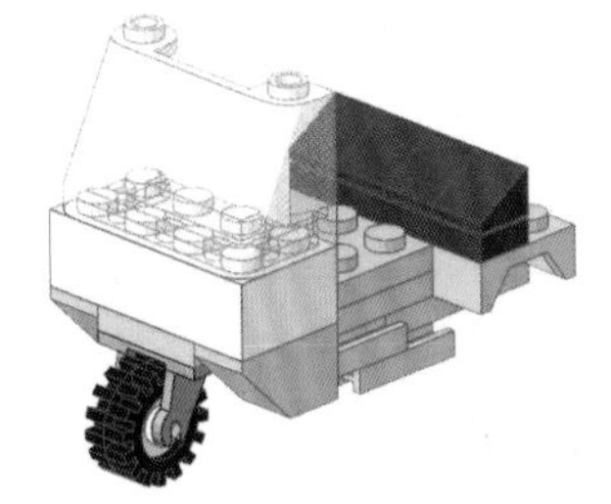

6

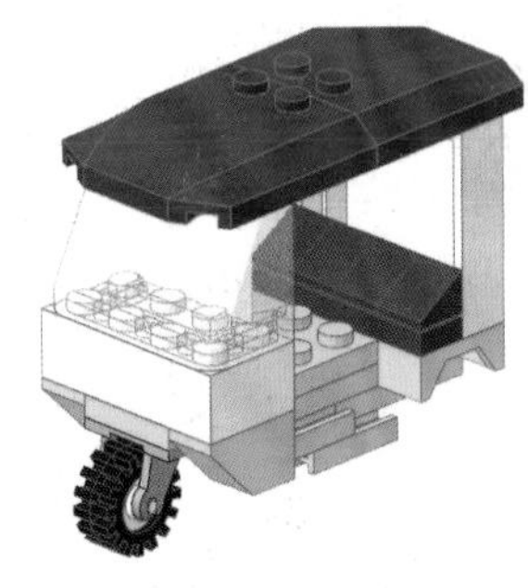

7

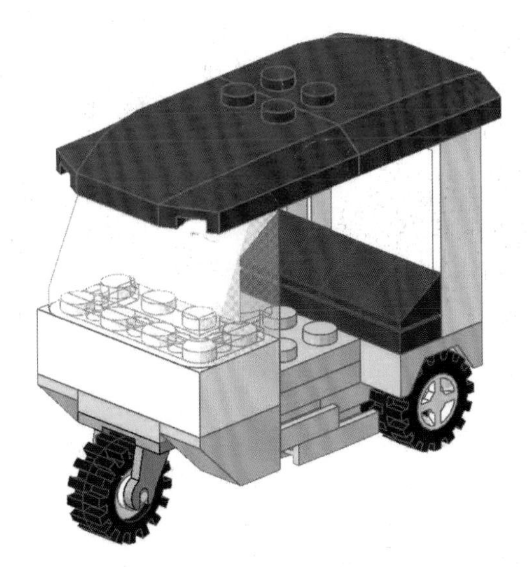

vw beetle

The Volkswagen Beetle, with its distinctive curves and round headlamps, has been a favorite since it was first mass-produced at the end of World War II. It is characterized by its bubble wheel arches and cute front design, which some say makes the car look like it has a smiling face! It was such an important car that it came in fourth in the 1999 Car of the Century competition. We have recreated our Beetle by using a variety of small, curved slopes, allowing us to showcase the car's curves.

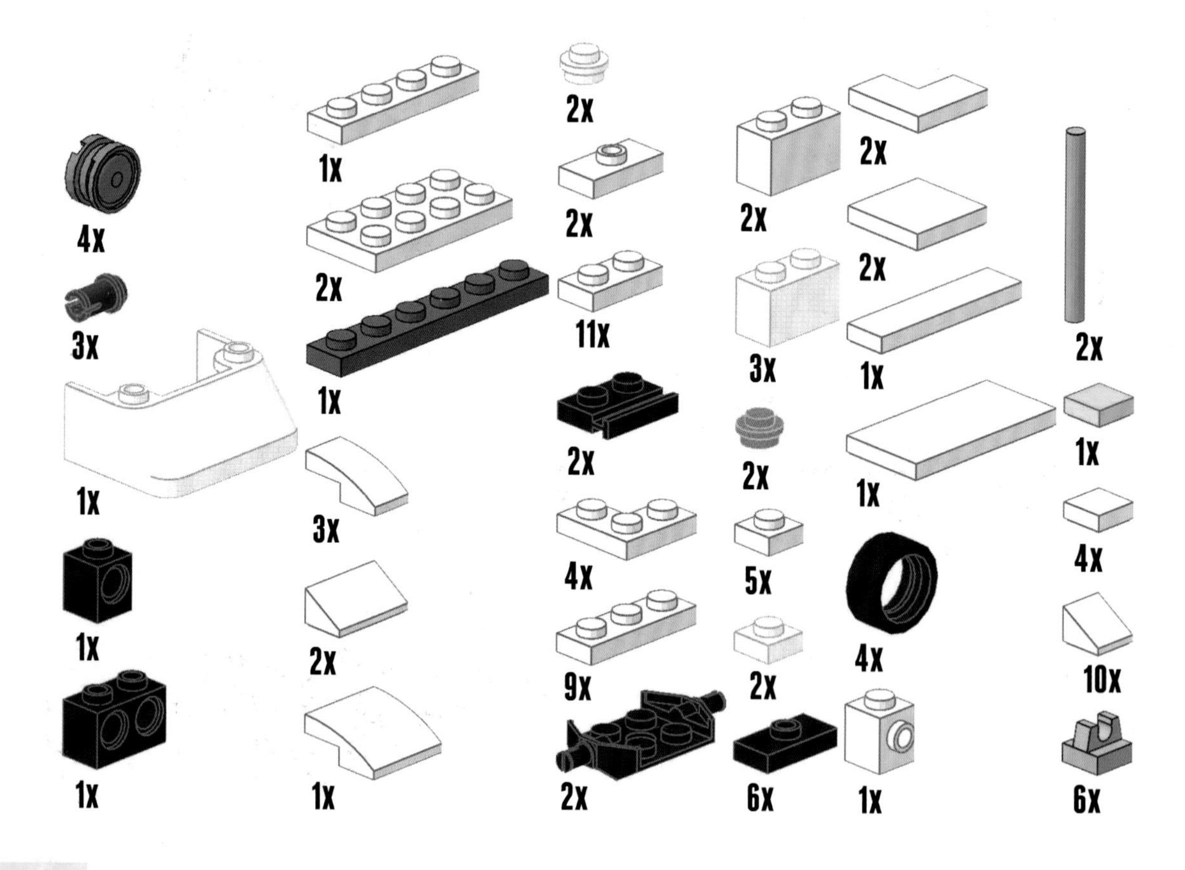

1

2

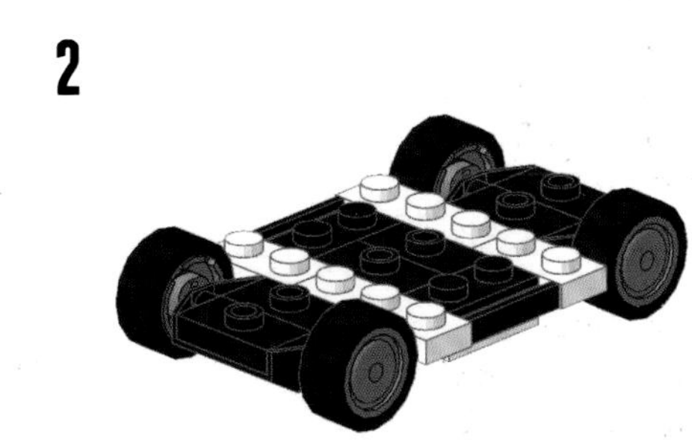

3

4

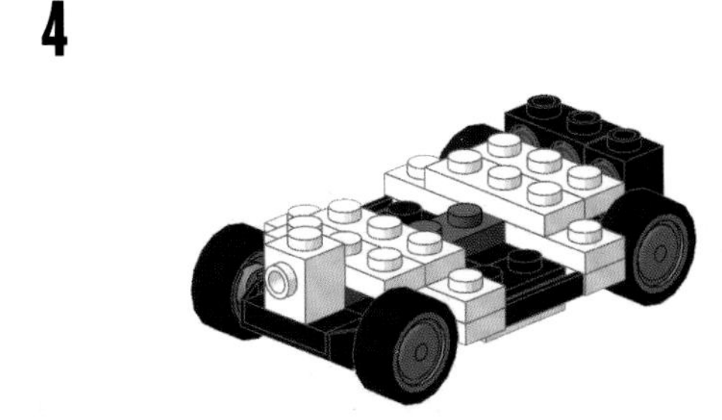

5

6

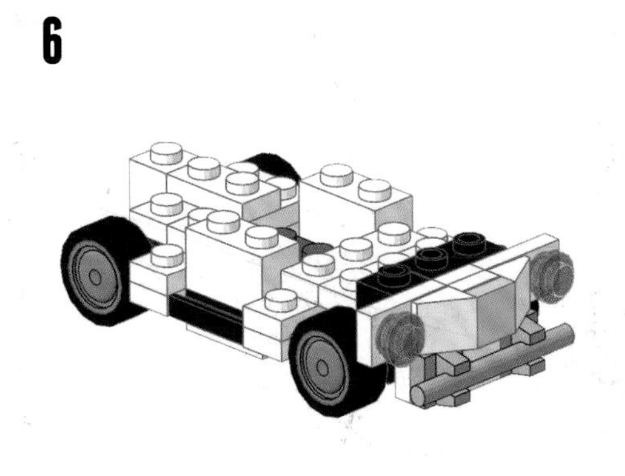

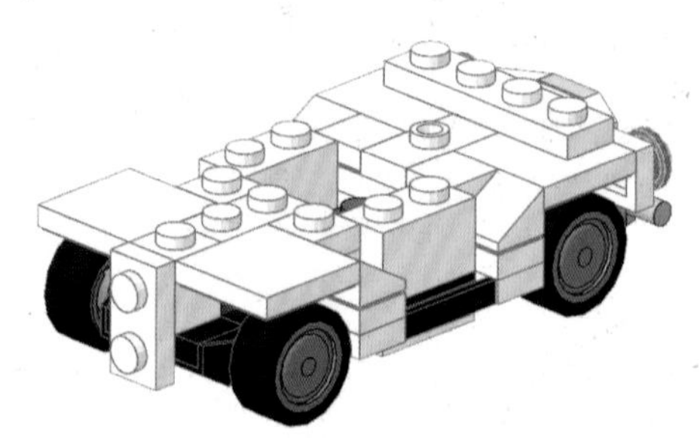

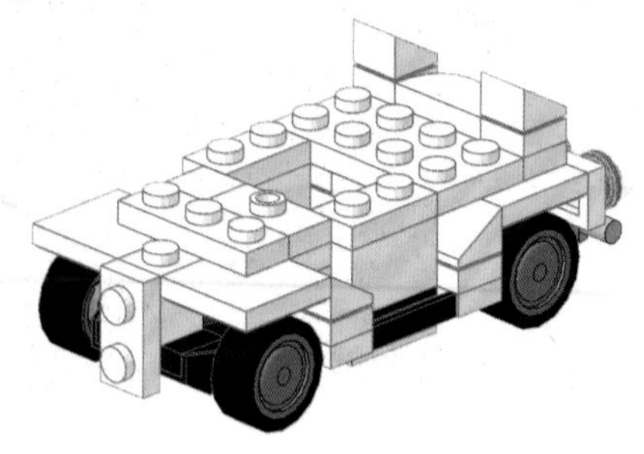

9

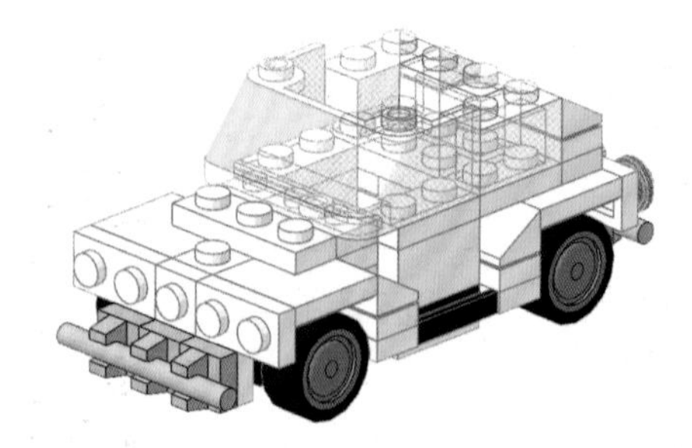

10

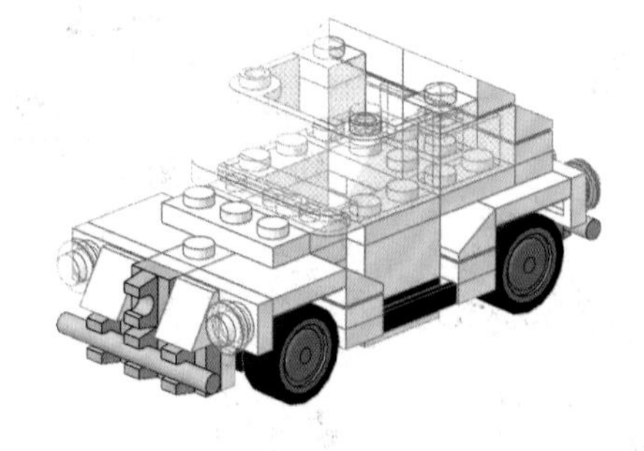

11

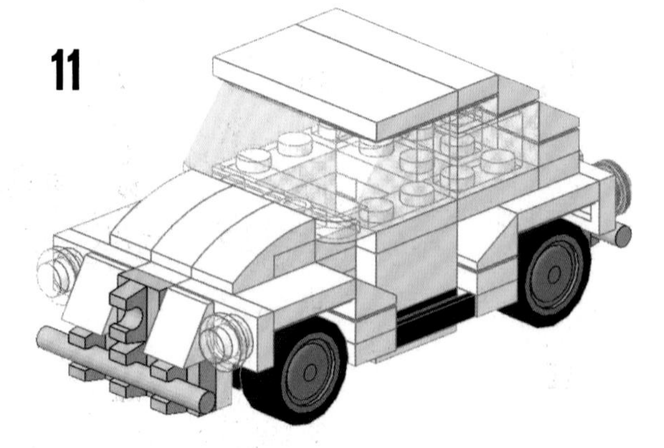

vintage car

American cars in the 1960s were known for their flamboyant tail fins and chrome accents. Our red car is based on the classic red Cadillac, with its long, sweeping hood and curved pop-up windshield. We've used 1 x 1 bricks, with one stud on the side, and some small wedge plates to represent the fins. The tail lights are then attached to the back of the car using upward brackets. The mini-fig binoculars give us the perfect shape for our typical 1960s-style headlights. We've used four of them, with 1 x 2 plates-with-rail to give us the iconic front styling.

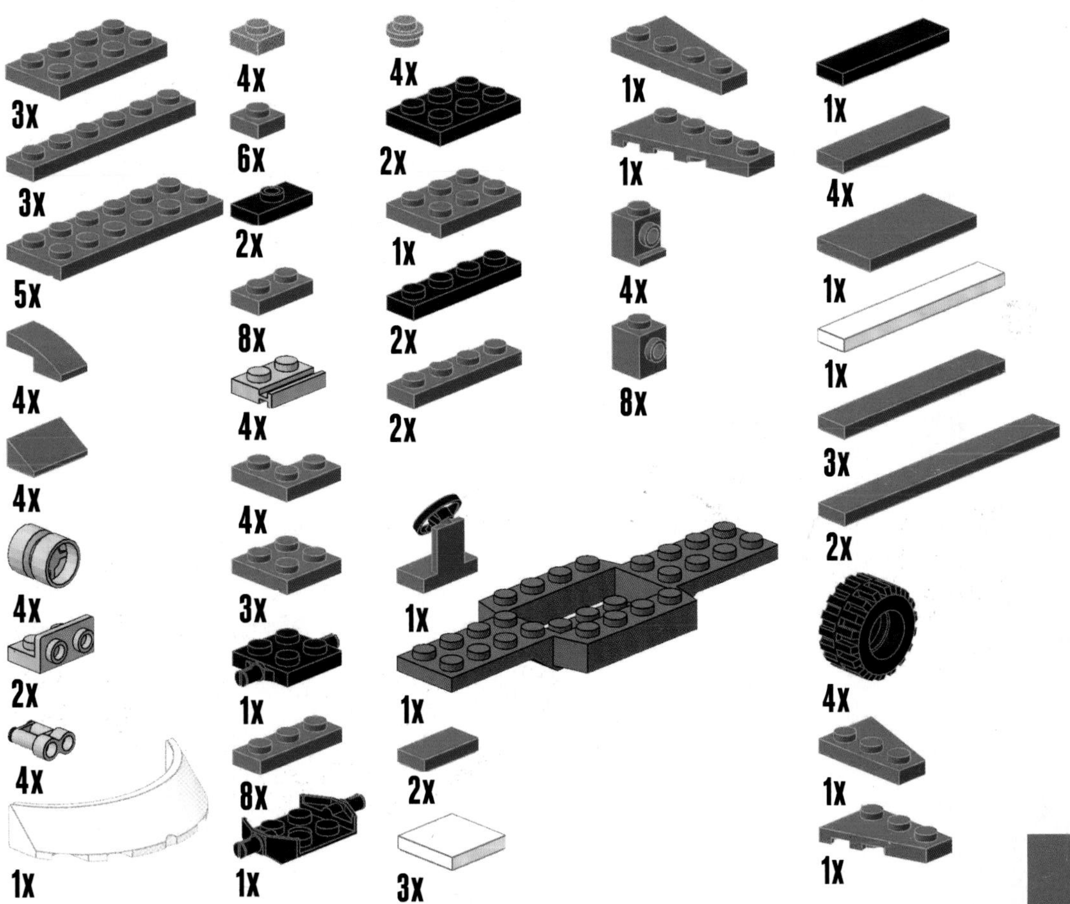

1

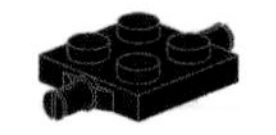

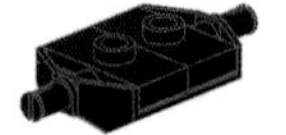

2

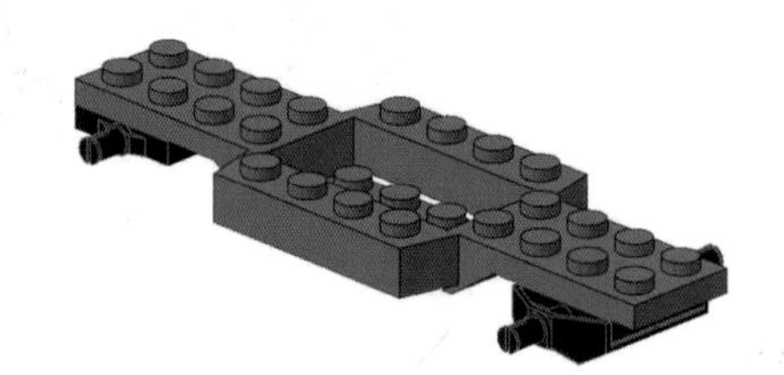

3

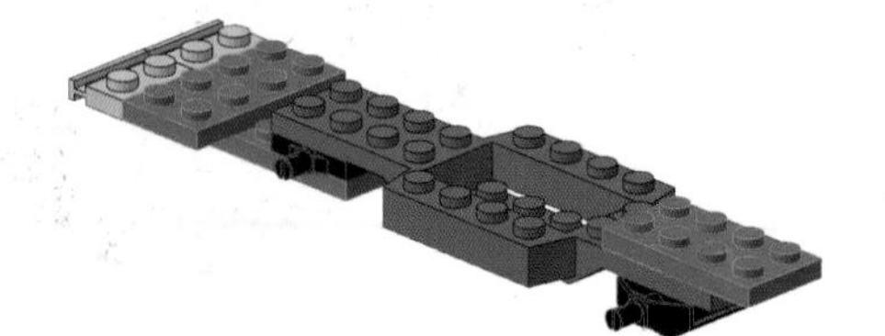

4

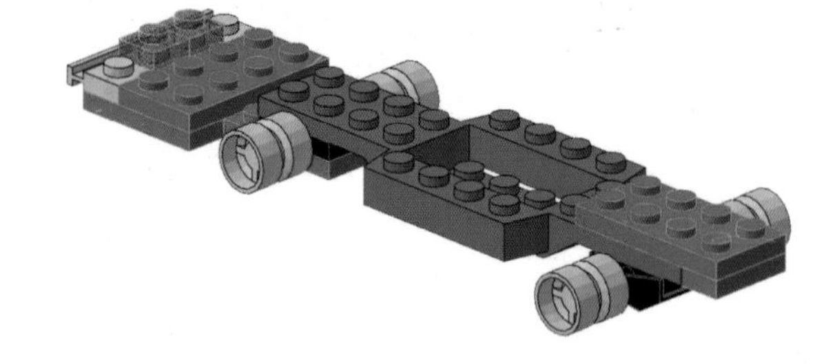

5

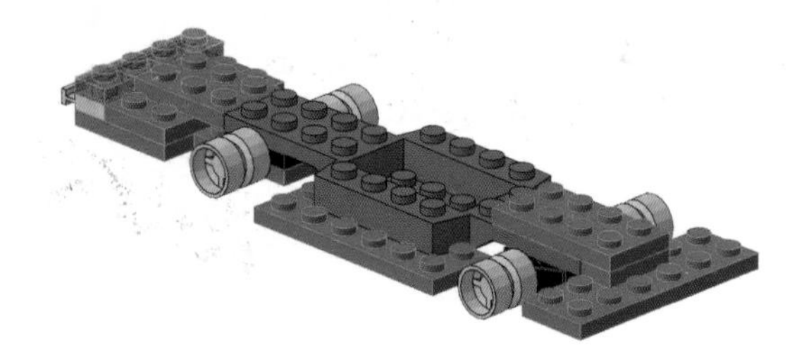

6

7

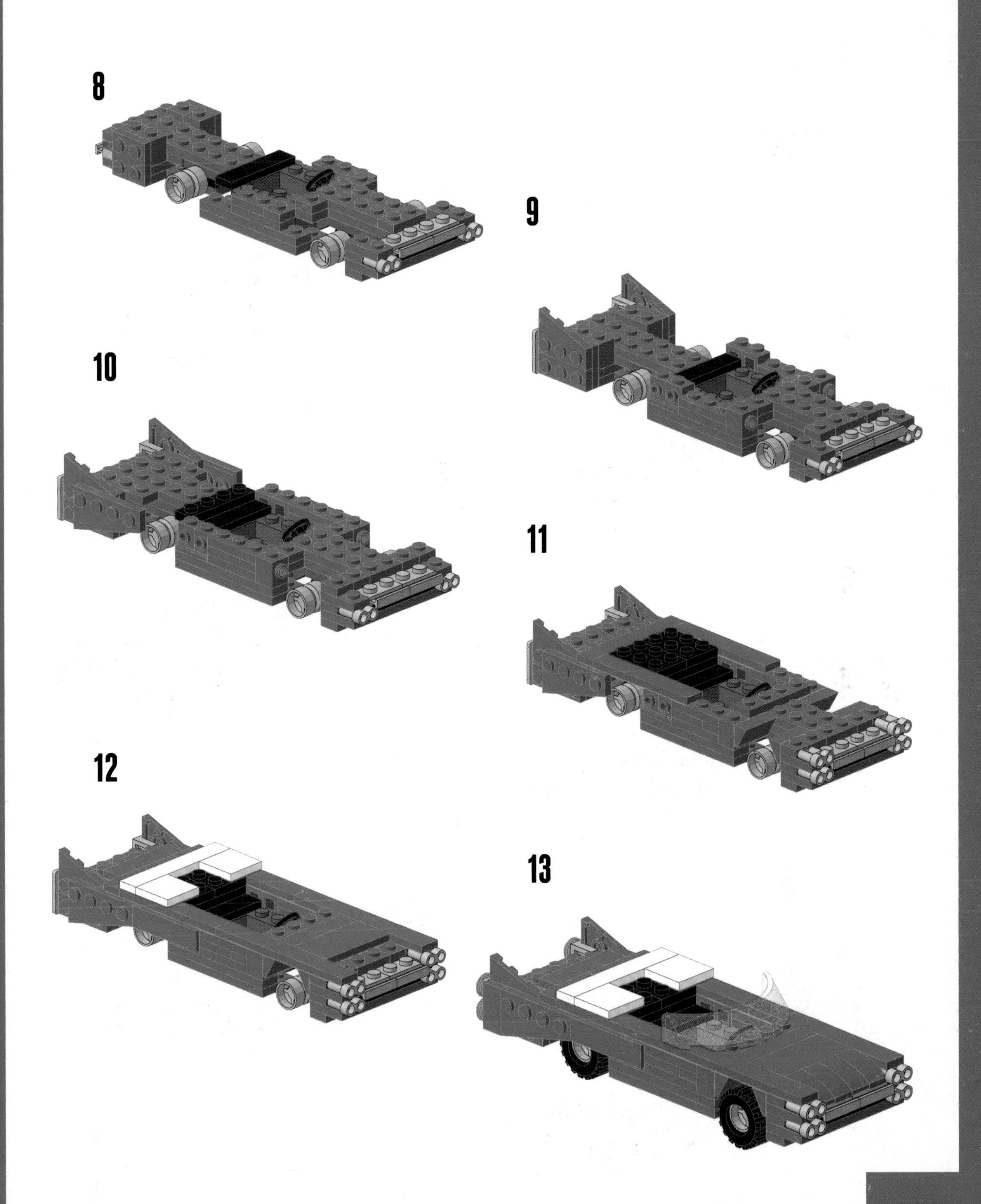
8
9
10
11
12
13

flying car

The car of the future? One day maybe we'll all be gliding through the air on four wheels and two wings instead of driving on the roads. This car is a glimpse into what might be, with its graceful, scalloped wings and retro-styled hood. A stack of 3 x 4 double-wedge plates creates a comfortable and safe driver's cab, while a transparent panel for the windshield protects the driver from the elements. A four-long bar with 1 x 1 tile clips and 1 x 1 transparent yellow round plates as headlamps completes the car's steampunk look.

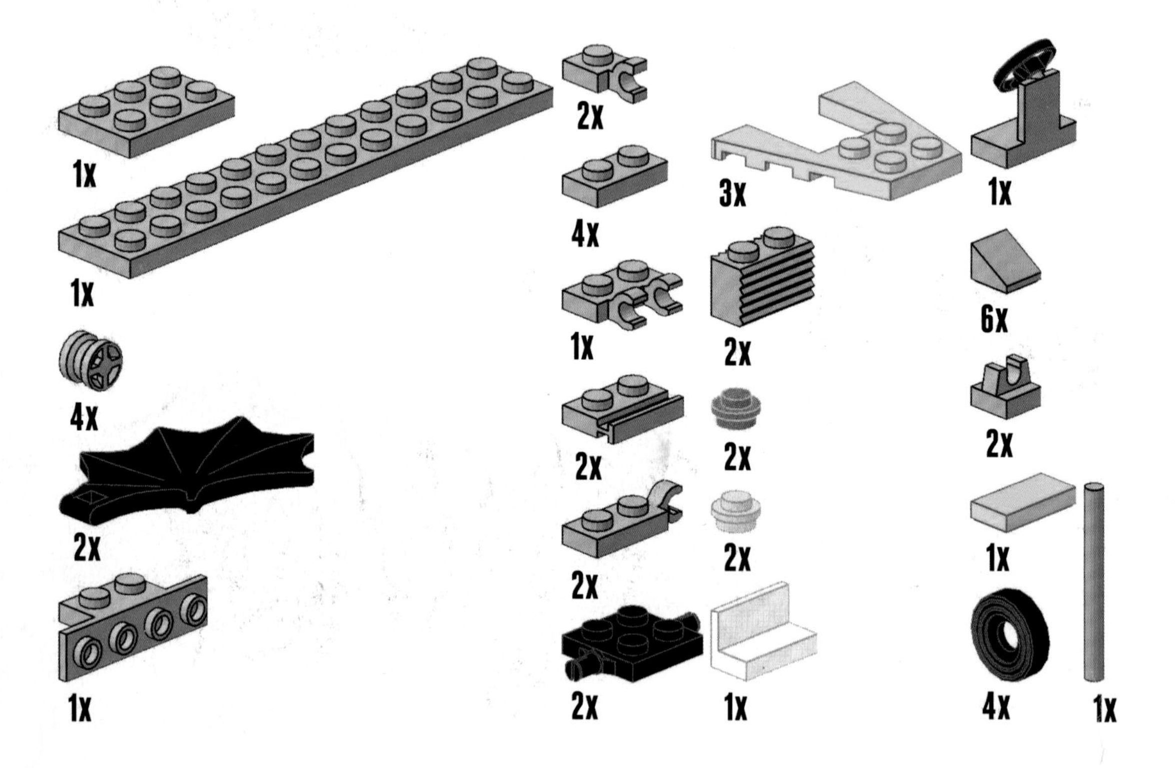

1

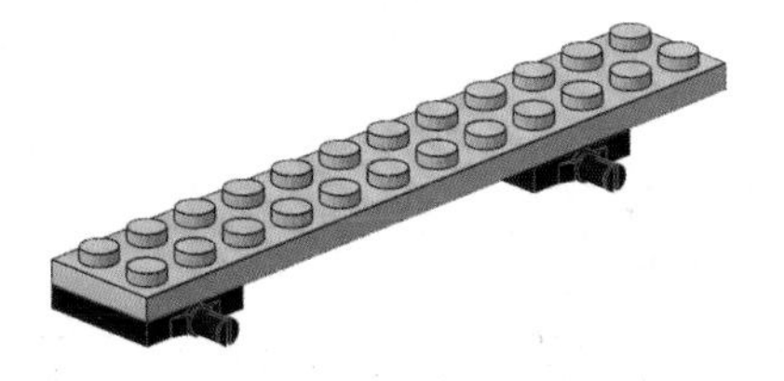

2

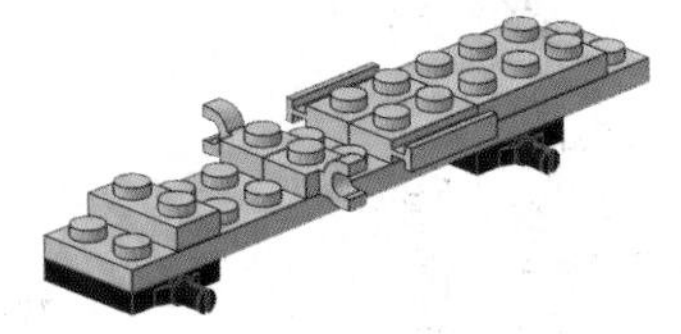

3

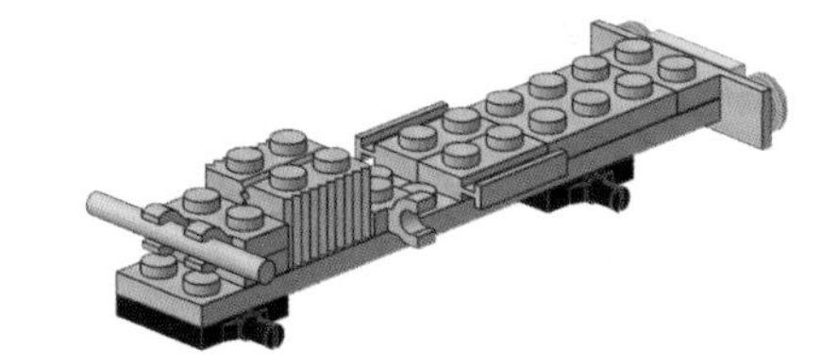

4

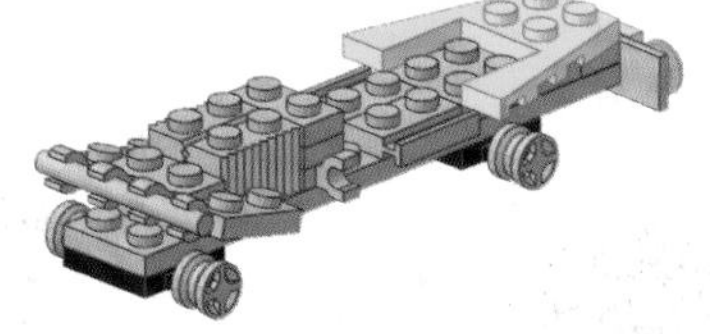

5

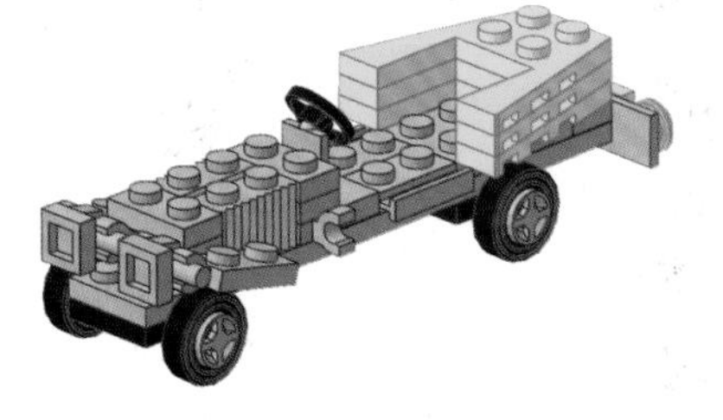

6

go kart

A go kart is a small, four-wheeled vehicle designed to stick to the asphalt when zipping around the racetrack. They come in all shapes and sizes, from the simplest gravity-driven soap-box racers to the more complex superkarts with powerful engines or electric motors. Most go karts only have space for the driver, but some models can accommodate a passenger. Our go kart uses a sturdy chassis piece to allow the body to be close to the ground. We have used a downward bracket to allow us to place a curved slope at 90 degrees to the chassis to create the bumper.

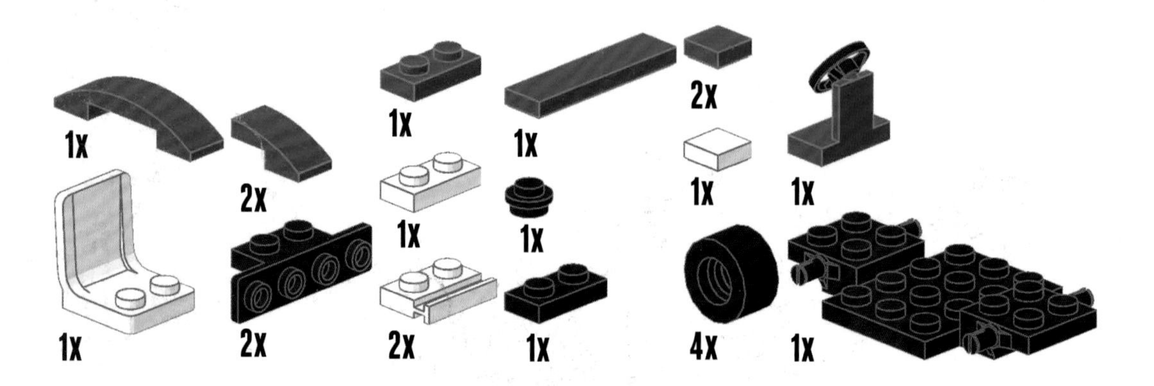

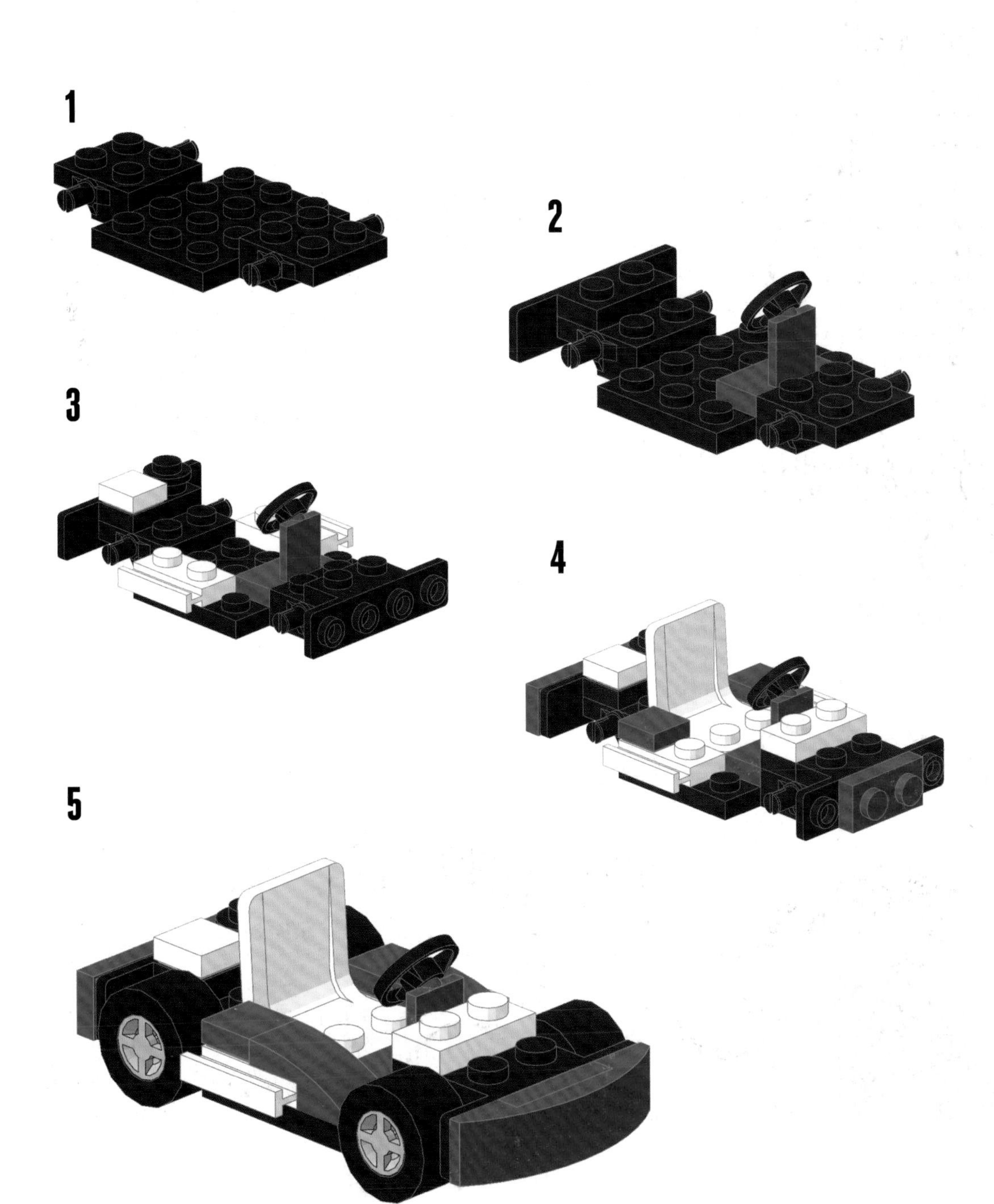
1
2
3
4
5

moon buggy

If you're flying to the moon, you need more than just your average car to get around! This archetypal moon buggy was used on several of the Apollo moon missions in the early 1970s. It was designed to carry a couple of astronauts, their equipment, and the samples they collected. As the moon buggies don't get packed up again for transport home, there are several of them still up there! The fat tires of our buggy are a different shape than most so they can negotiate the rocky surface of the moon.

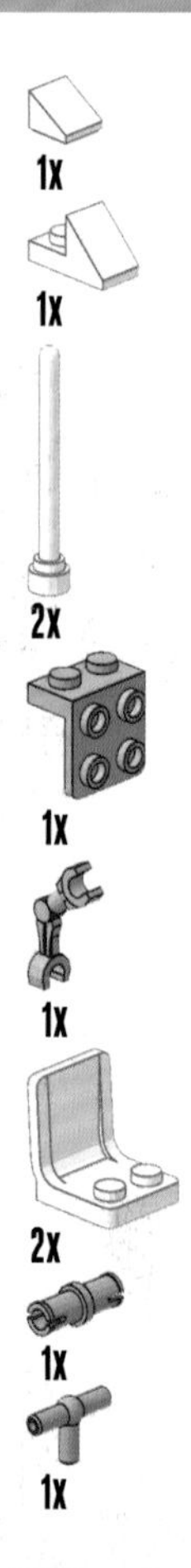

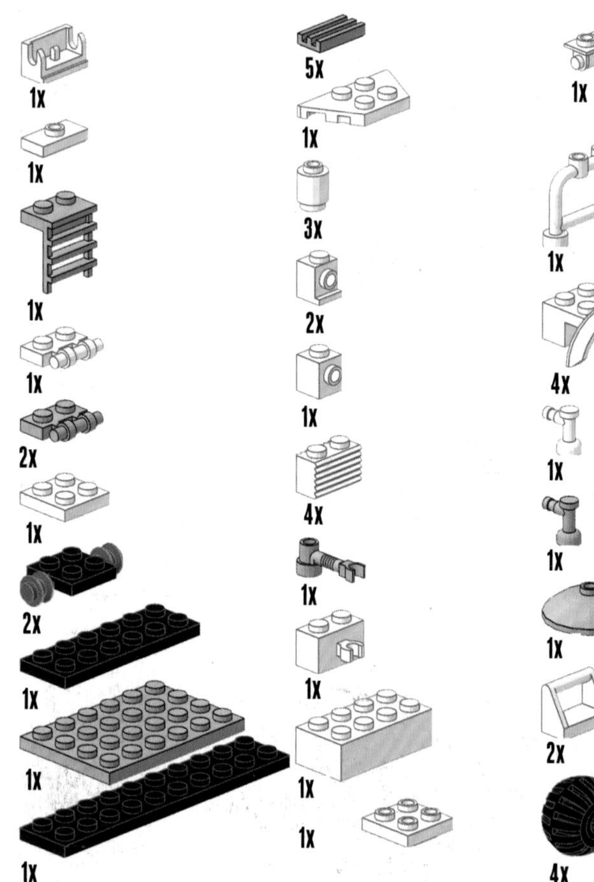

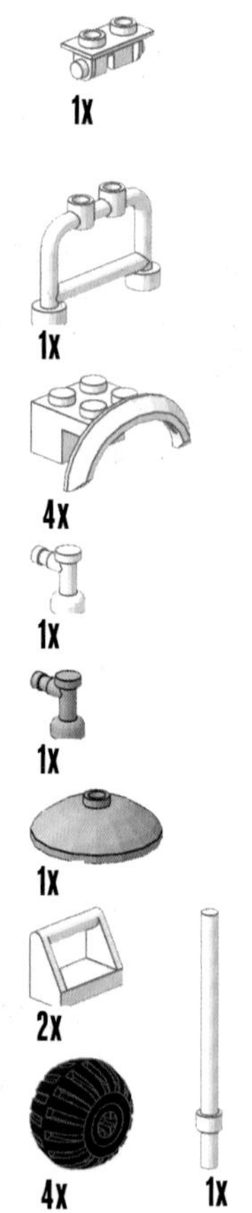

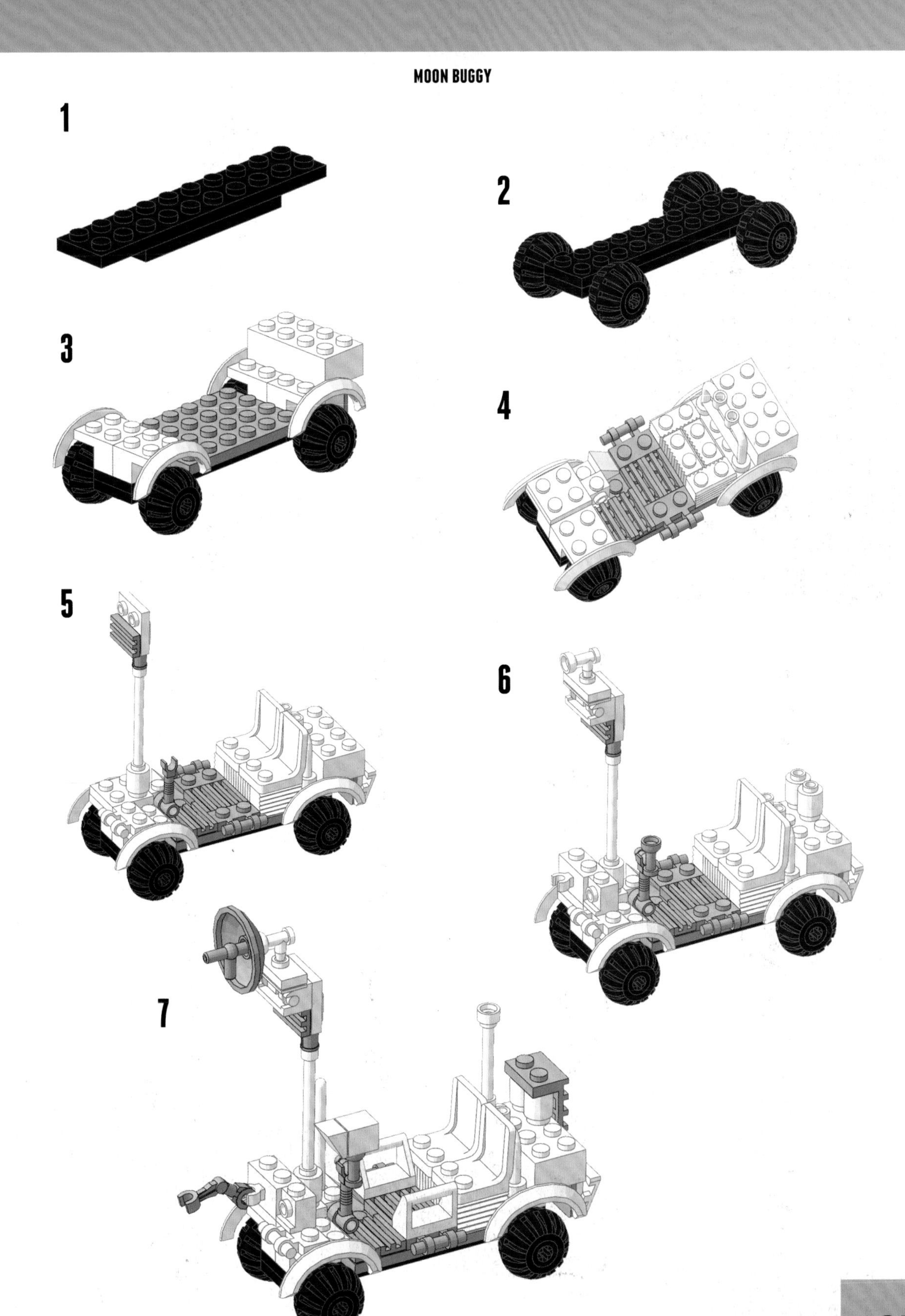
1
2
3
4
5
6
7

double-decker bus

All aboard! Double-decker buses—like the famous London Routemaster—have seating on two levels, with enough space to transport up to 70 people in one go. They're used as tour buses in big cities such as New York, but our model is based on the London bus with its trademark bright red. We've chosen to make it to mini-scale, using different colored plates to pick out the windows and advertising posters on the side of the bus.

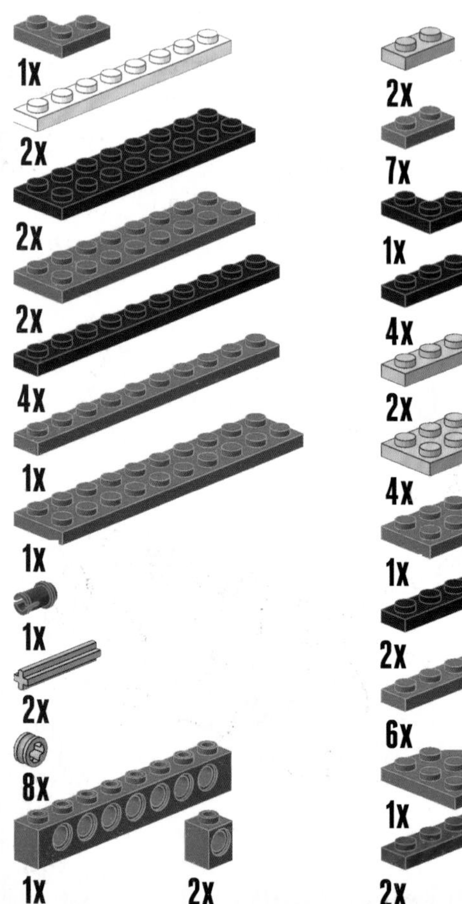

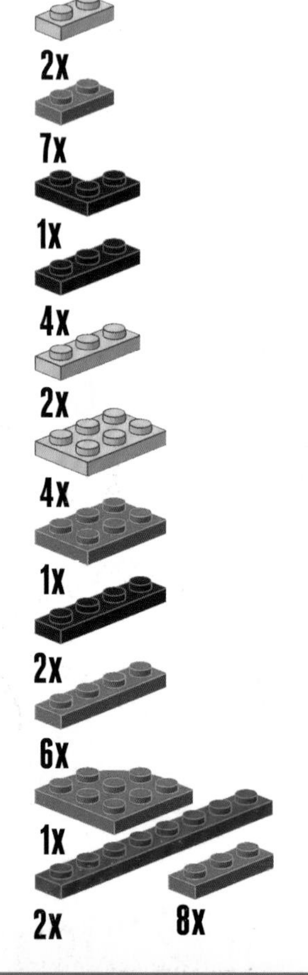

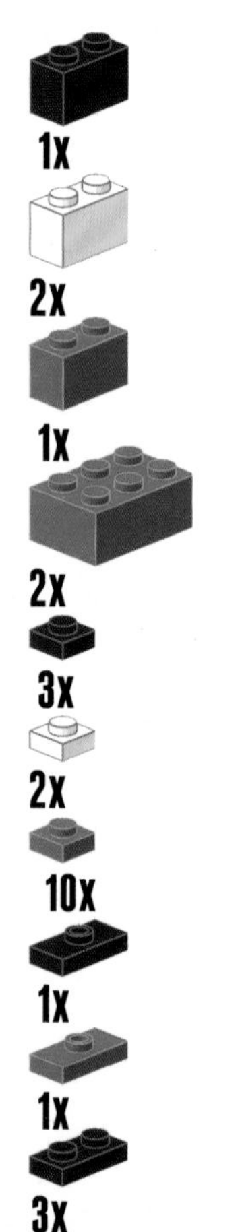

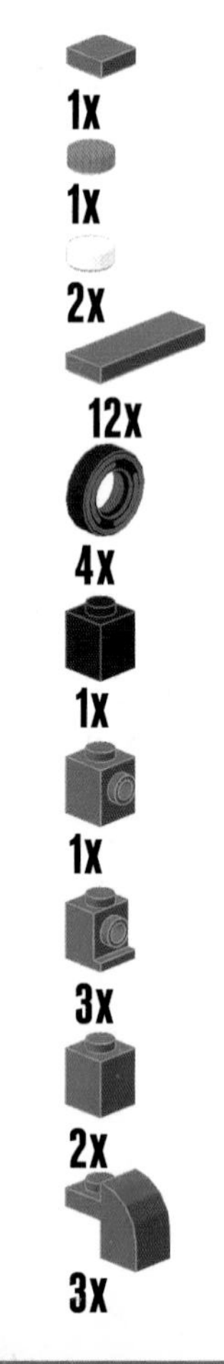

1

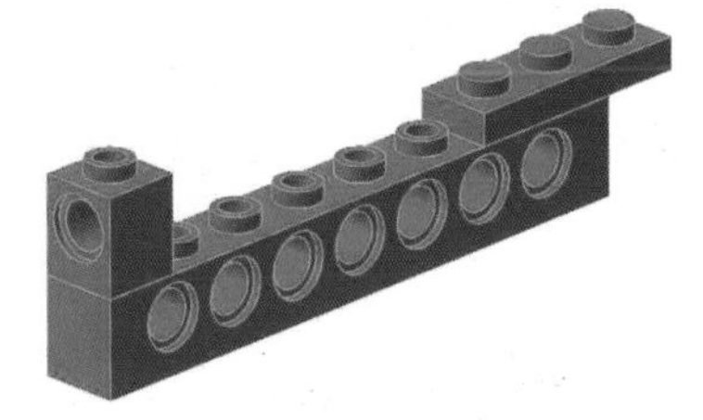

2

3

4

5

6

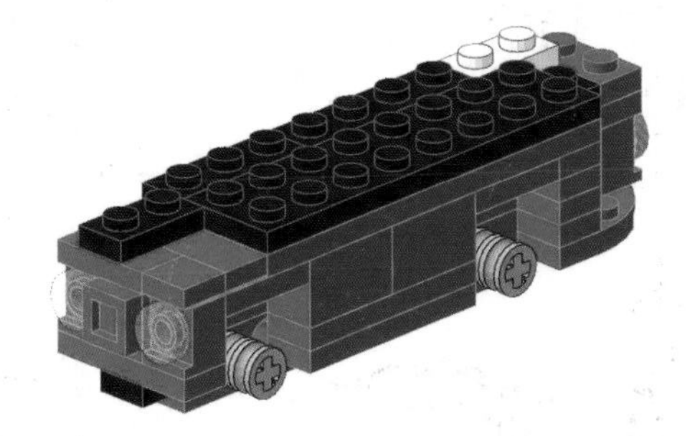

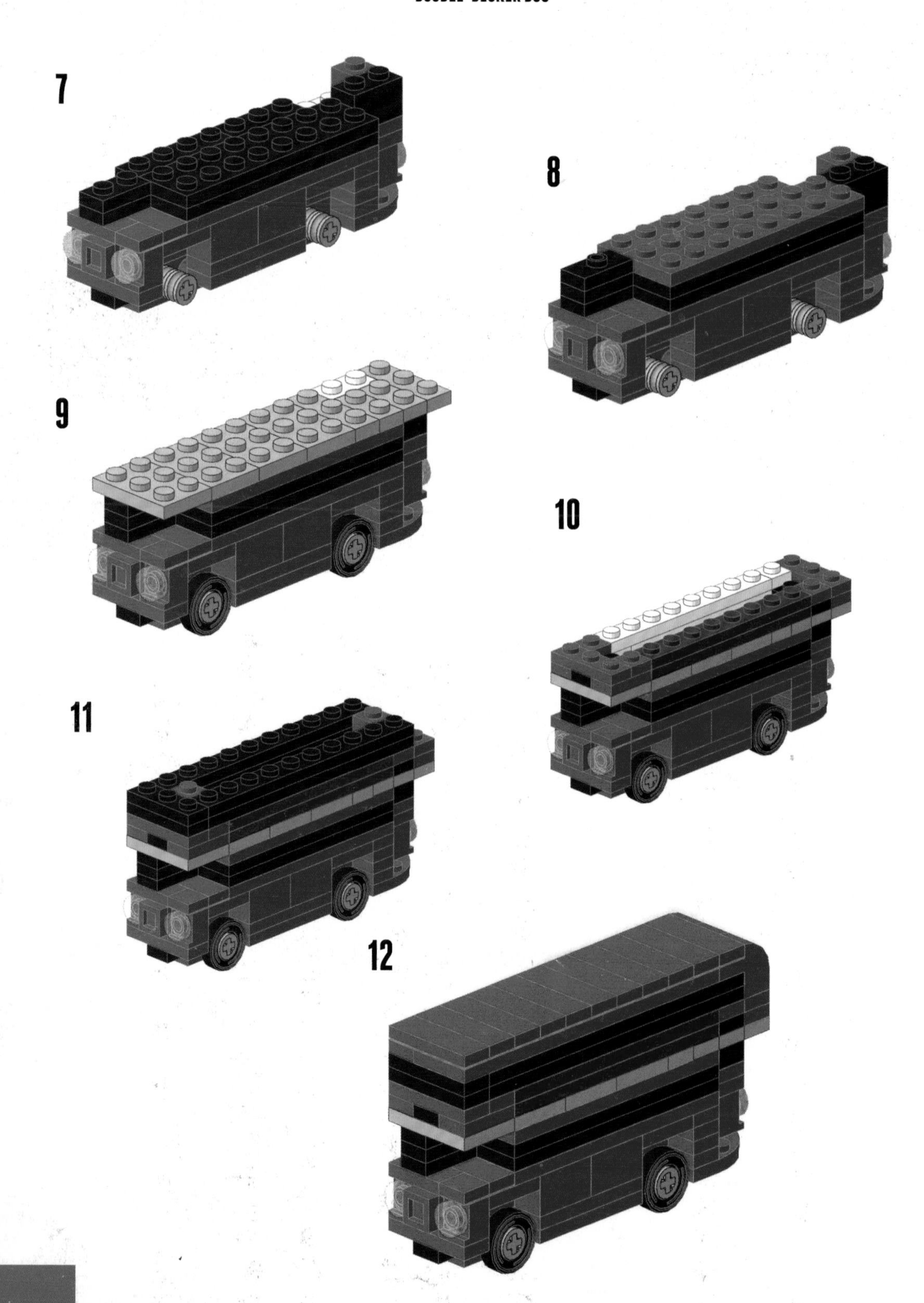
7
8
9
10
11
12

ice cream truck

Summer is here! When you hear the chimes of the ice cream truck's song, you know a sweet, ice-cold treat is waiting for you. Our van is decorated with both chocolate and vanilla ice cream on sale, using the ice cream cone piece with 1 x 1 round plates for the color. To create the serving hatch, we've built a large sliding window made from the 1 x 4 x 3 window frame. The shape of the roof is made by using 1 x 4 curved bricks. And don't forget the interior—you need a freezer to store all that delicious ice cream!

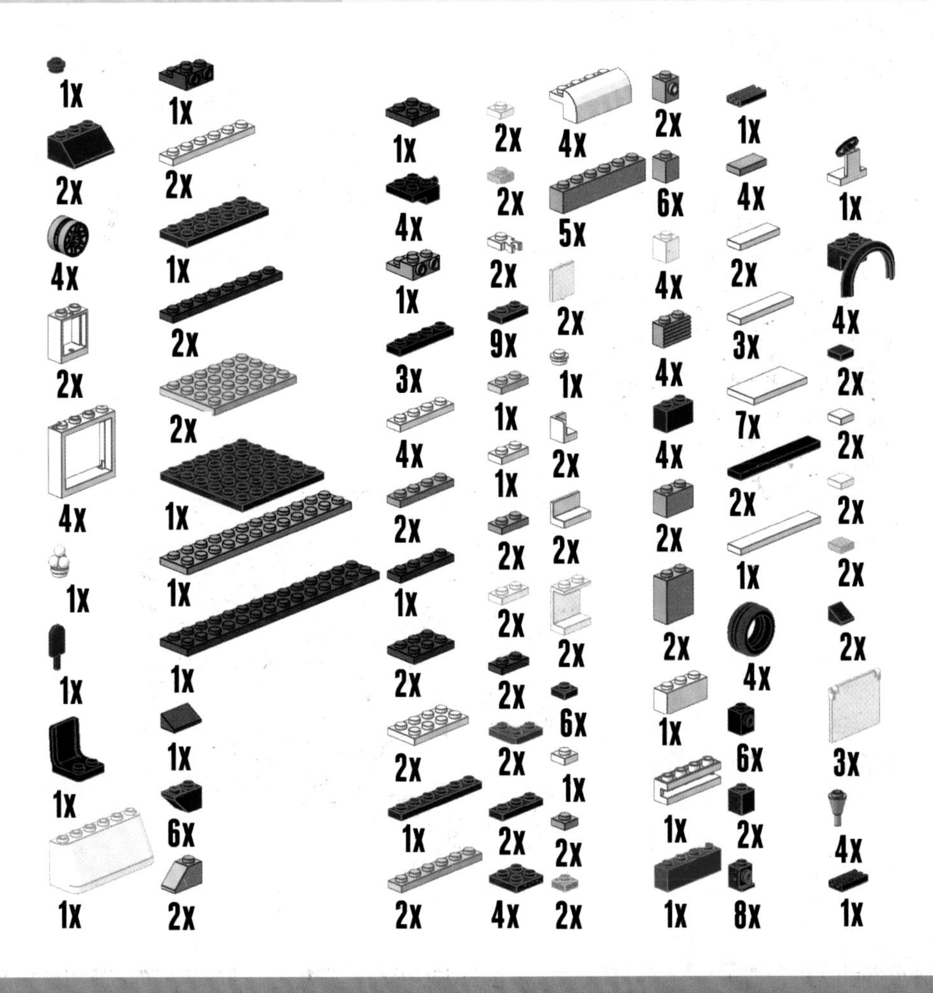

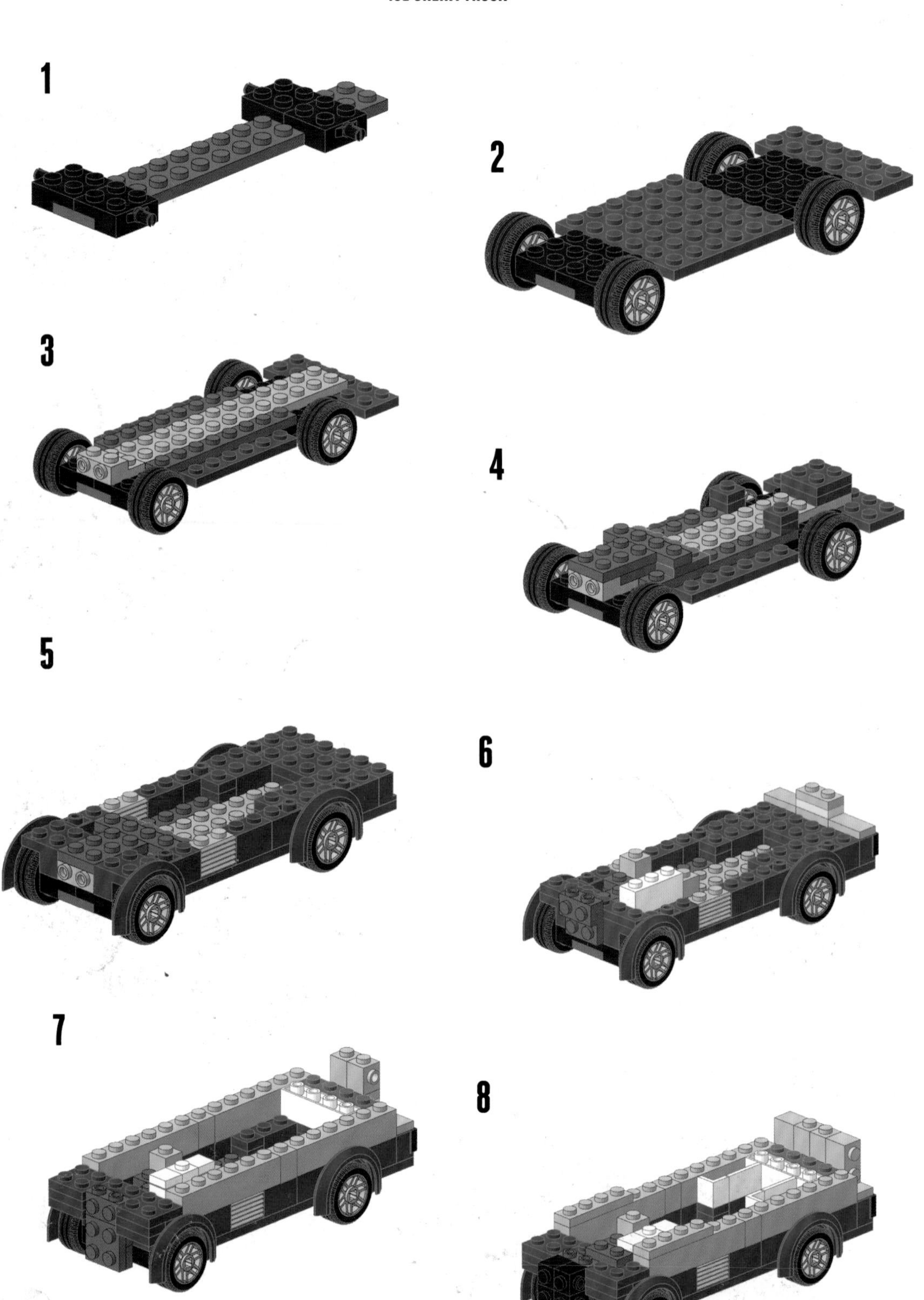
1
2
3
4
5
6
7
8

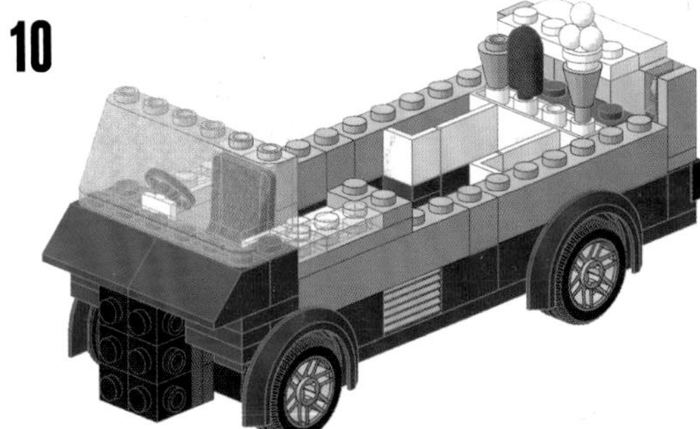

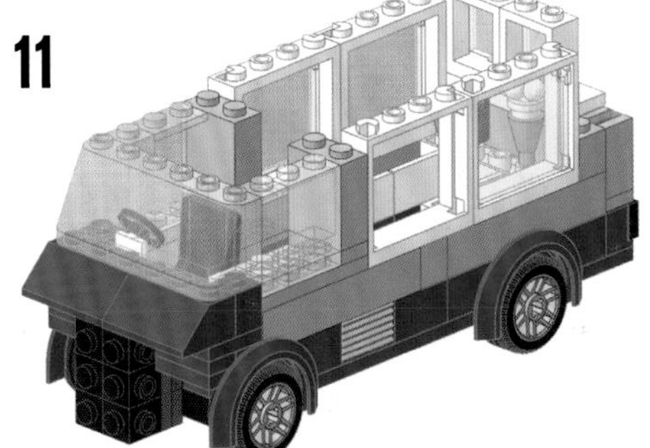

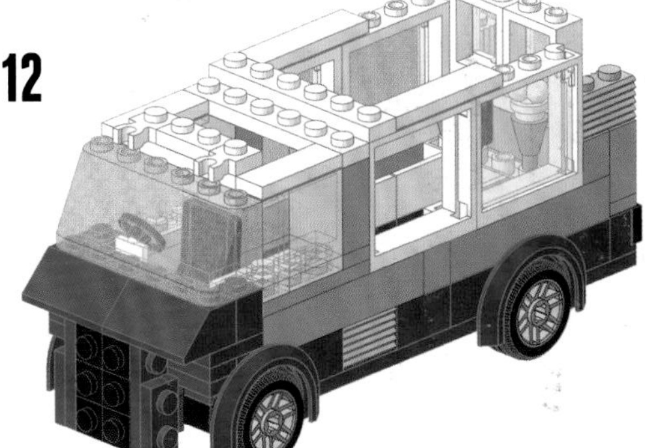

13

14

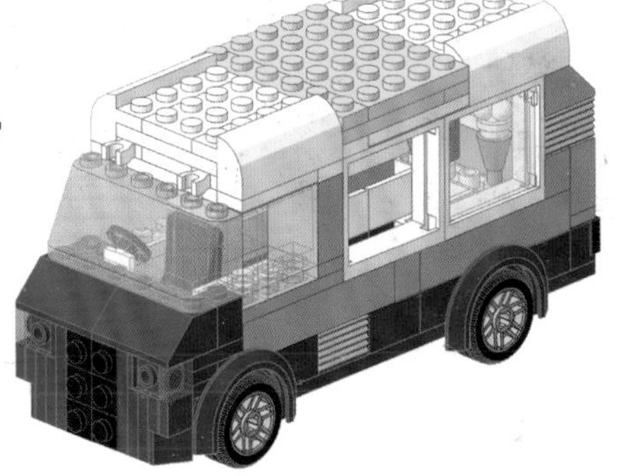

15

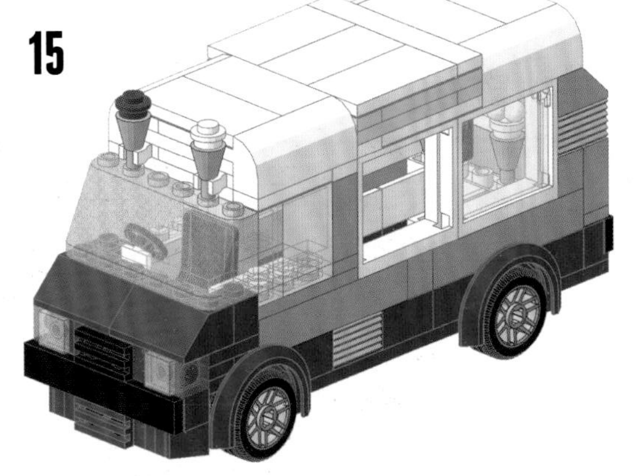

jeep

We've based our Jeep on the Willys MB, a four-wheel drive utility vehicle that was a major part of the backbone of the US Army transport from 1941 onward. It was also a common sight in TV programs and films. The boxy shape of the Jeep lends itself well to LEGO®, and we've used that in the simple shape of the 1 x 4 transparent brick and topping-off tile for the fold-down windscreen. The spare wheel is held onto the back of the Jeep by 1 x 2 to 2 x 2 downward brackets and a 2 x 2 tile with Technic pin.

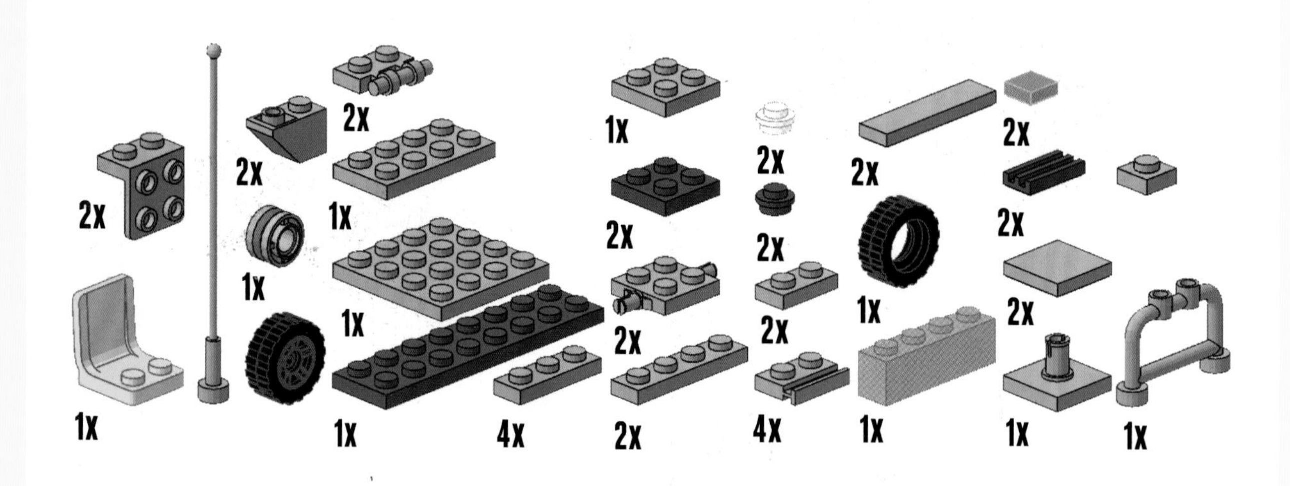

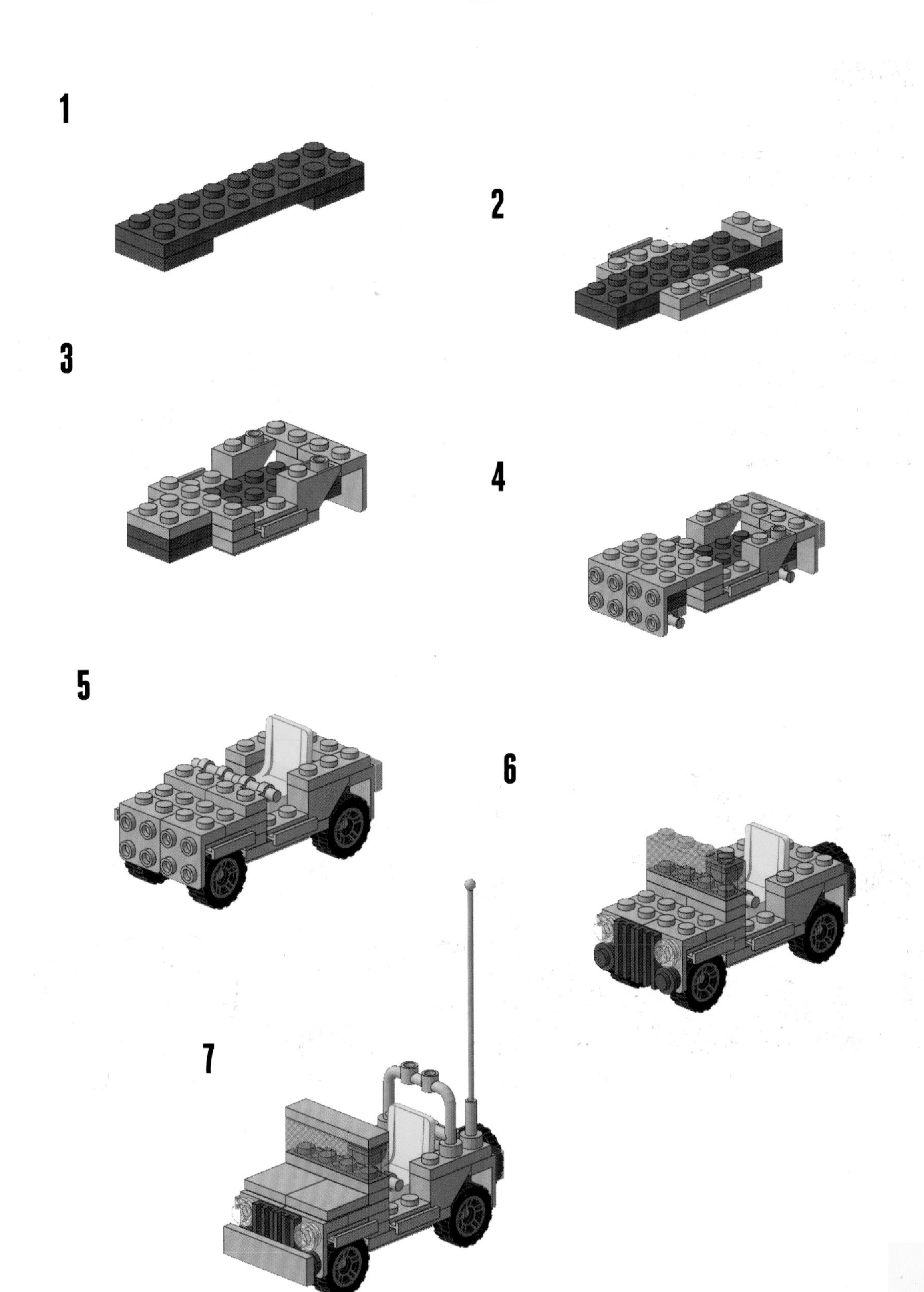
1
2
3
4
5
6
7

hummer

Based on the U.S. military M998 Humvee, the Hummer is an SUV known for its square shape and imposing size. They are largely equipped to go off-road, with fat tires and high ground-clearance. The square edges of LEGO® plates and bricks lend themselves very well to the box shape of the Hummer bodywork. We've used four long bars in 1 x 1 tile clips to give our model a chunky roof-rack. The same bars threaded through 1 x 1 plates recreate the bull bar on the front.

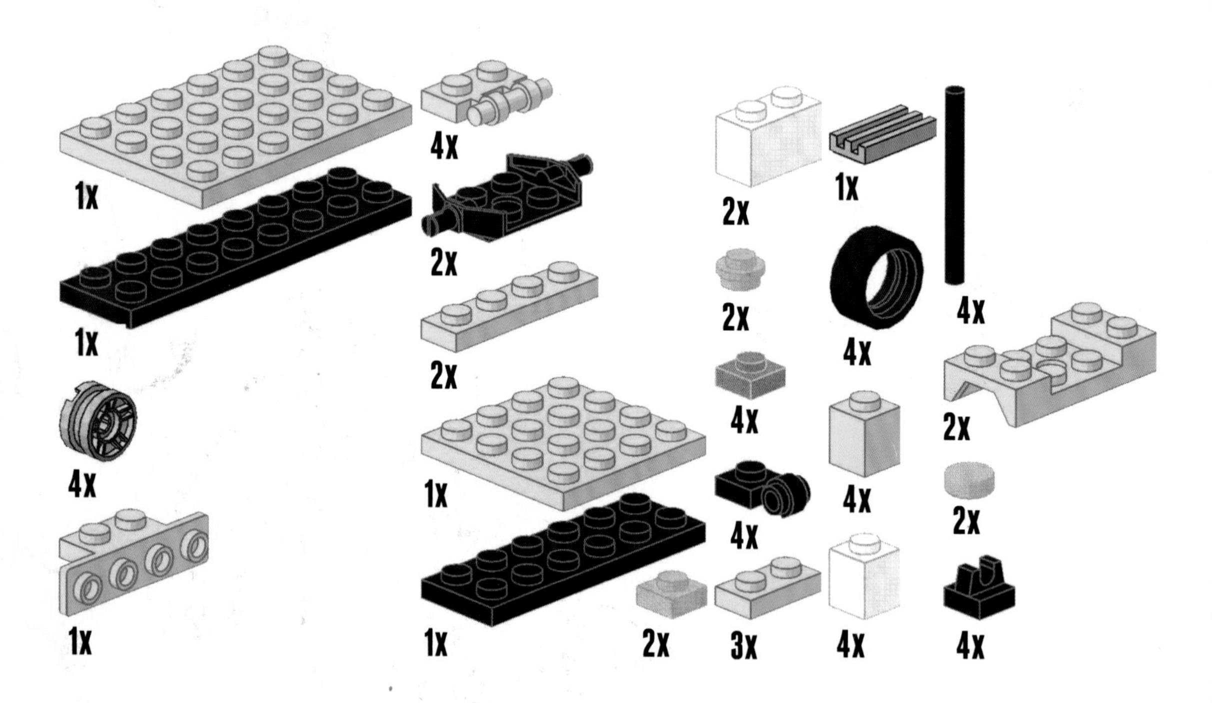

HUMMER

1

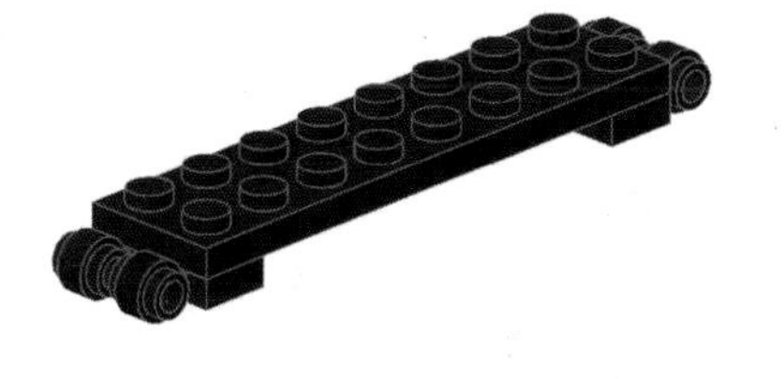

2

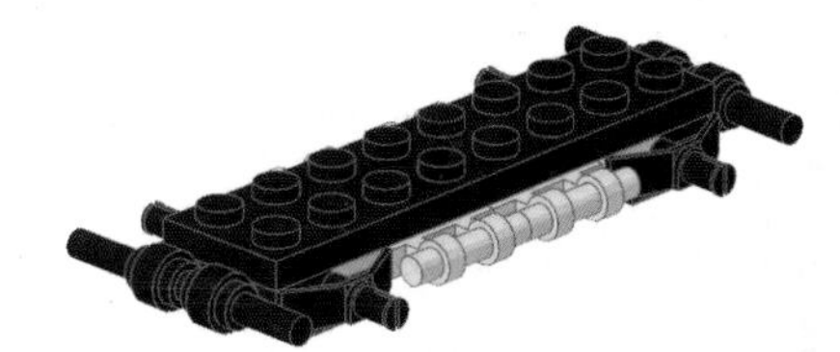

3

4

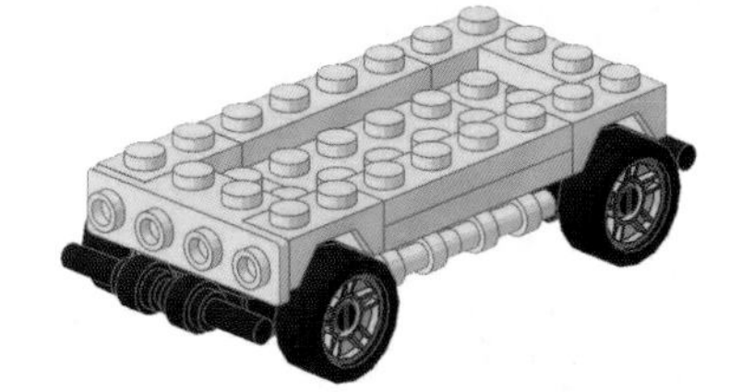

5

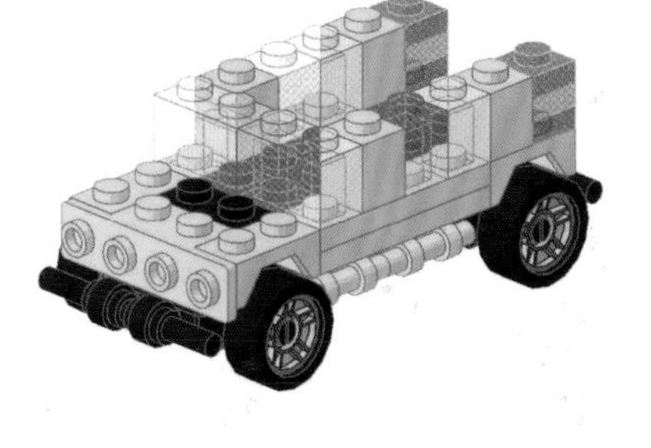

6

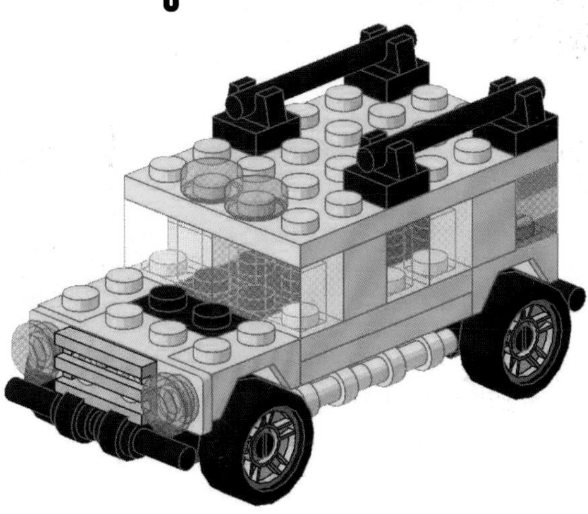

credits

Warren Elsmore, based in Edinburgh, U.K., is an artist in LEGO® bricks and a lifelong fan of them. He has been in love with the little plastic bricks since the age of four and now spends his days creating amazing models out of them. After 15 years in a successful IT career, in 2012 Warren moved to working full time with LEGO bricks. He now helps multinational companies to realize their own dreams in plastic. Warren's bestselling first book, *Brick City*, was released in 21 languages to widespread critical acclaim, and has been followed by a range of books recreating famous places, objects, and historical events in LEGO. His models have always attracted great press coverage—in fact, thanks to the British Antarctic Survey, one of his models has even made it as far as the South Pole! Exhibitions of Warren's *Brick City* and *Brick Wonders* have toured museums and galleries throughout the United Kingdom, entertaining hundreds of thousands of children of all ages. In 2015, Warren co-launched BRICK—the largest LEGO fan event in the United Kingdom, and one of the largest in the world. For more information, visit *warrenelsmore.com*.

Teresa "Kitty" Elsmore, who researched and co-wrote this book, was a LEGO fan as a child and continues to enjoy creating models today. She is passionate about including all the little details that bring a scene to life. Since their marriage in 2005, Teresa and Warren have collaborated on a number of projects and now run a successful business together, getting paid to make models from LEGO.

Guy Bagley always enjoyed model making as a hobby, but it became his career after he earned an industrial model-making degree at the University of Hertfordshire, U.K. After a short spell in the film and TV industry, Guy moved into architectural model making, and finally to toy design with companies such as Mattel and Hasbro. Guy moved to the LEGO group in 1992, where he was involved in planning and building LEGOLAND® Windsor. Next, he became Lead Designer and Model Shop Manager working on new LEGOLAND Theme Parks and LEGOLAND Discovery Centers around the globe. After 23 years he is now pursuing new challenges with Warren Elsmore's team, and has never looked back!

Alastair Disley is a professional LEGO builder, architectural historian, and musician. Previously a university lecturer, he lives in the Scottish Borders, U.K. with his young family.